THE MAKING OF
TOWN GARDENS

The Making of Town Gardens

DEBORAH KELLAWAY

Photographs by
ANDREW LAWSON

Garden plans by
HESTER ROBINSON

MACMILLAN
LONDON

First published 1990 by
MACMILLAN LONDON LIMITED
4 Little Essex Street London WC2R 3LF
and Basingstoke

Associated companies in Auckland, Delhi, Dublin, Gaborone,
Hamburg, Harare, Hong Kong, Johannesburg, Kuala Lumpur,
Lagos, Manzini, Melbourne, Mexico City, Nairobi, New York,
Singapore and Tokyo

ISBN 0-333-52623-6

A CIP catalogue record for this book is available from the
British Library

Typeset by Matrix, 21 Russell Street, London WC2

Printed in Hong Kong

To Lucy G.
and Lucy K.

Contents

Contents

List of Illustrations

List of Plates

Acknowledgements

My thanks are due to those who have kindly given me permission to reproduce copyright material in this book: to Faber and Faber Ltd for lines from T. S. Eliot's 'Rhapsody on a Windy Night' (*Collected Poems, 1909–1962*); to Curtis Brown Ltd on behalf of the author's estate for the quotation from one of V. Sackville West's 'In Your Garden' articles; to John Murray (Publishers) Ltd for the lines from John Betjeman's *Collected Poems*: and to Martin Secker & Warburg for the extract from Collette's *Flowers and Fruit*.

I owe a special debt to the writings of Geoffrey and Susan Jellicoe: in particular to Geoffrey Jellicoe's *Guelph Lectures on Landscape Design* and to *The New Small Garden* by Lady Allen of Hurtwood and Susan Jellicoe.

But my deepest gratitude goes to the gardeners – my friends and neighbours – who have tirelessly shown me their gardens, lent me lists, plans, notes and photographs, and given me free rein to write whatever I please.

I

In an Australian City

Many a garden has left its memory
with me. Almost all were to my liking,
except those that were too young or were
up to me to plant.

Colette, 'Flowers and Fruit'

Behind the yellow stucco neo-Georgian house was a rectangular garden, wider than it was long. Down each side went a border and down the middle a path of paving slabs with grass between. Halfway along this path, and thus in the middle of the garden, was a circular feature: a rose-bed divided into four segments by crossing paths. The roses were standards, growing out of bare earth. At the bottom of the garden was a wooden paling fence, and beyond that a vacant building site. This was my parents' garden in a prosperous suburb of Melbourne in the 1920s.

Nothing here was a surprise. Everything was symmetrical and straight. Between the side borders and the central path were two lawns, each with a small lemon tree in it growing near the house. There were borders beneath the house verandahs with another path, at right angles to the first, separating them from the lawn. This path led through a gap in a screening cypress hedge to a depressing area called the yard. Here were two large green sheds, weatherboarded, one full of firewood called 'mallee roots', the other, padlocked, full of my grandmother's stored furniture and old cabin trunks. High above was a rotary

1

clothes-line called the whirligig. I was very small when I first knew this place.

There was a melancholy Scandinavian gardener called Chris, in waistcoat and shirtsleeves, who battled against nature in this garden and planted annuals out in rows, stiff bright red and yellow zinnias on one side, fat scented pink and puce stocks, mixed doubles and singles, on the other, with purple and pink asters behind, and bright little *Phlox drummondii* near the paths. I used to pull their flowers off and suck the sweet nectar from their tubes. There was also a succession of people called 'nurse' who took us for afternoon walks in the botanical gardens.

Melbourne's Botanic Gardens, designed by William Guilfoyle, are now renowned but seemed to me then a beautiful but wearisomely obligatory extension of the afternoons. There were huge spaces of lawn, vast and varied trees, hard-surfaced walks, a big lake where black swans sailed, and a cool, dark, frightening place where paths wound up and down through towering palms and tree ferns amongst ever-dripping water. There were mournful wooden shelters, gabled and empty save for long, uncomfortable benches to sit on when it rained.

One day my father bought the vacant block at the bottom of our garden, giving us an acre of land in all. The fence came down and Edna Walling was called in, Australia's answer to Gertrude Jekyll and her true descendant. She, too, was an artist; she did not like straight lines and neatness. She liked a romantic enhancement of nature, and she drew beautiful garden plans, tinted in watercolour. The first part of our garden, near the house, remained neat and prosy as before, but the second part, the new bit, became poetry, with ravishing little specimen trees in the grass, a weeping apple tree, a silver birch, and a curving path down one side, between flowing borders backed by an arcade of simply arched timber slats over which bright yellow jasmine was trained – not the winter jasmine of English gardens, but the exotic half-hardy *Jasminum grandiflorum*, an

Twin cypresses between the old garden and the new.

evergreen with summer flowers. The boundaries were planted out with shrubs and small trees, green- and purple-leafed, crab apples and plums.

To articulate the joint between the two gardens, the straight and the curving, the old and the new, she devised her inspired stroke: two slender Italian cypress trees, *Cupressus sempervirens* 'Gracilis', placed centrally at the bottom of the main path, with a sundial set on paving between them. There was a third, slightly thicker cypress a little to one side, as if to show that asymmetry must temper symmetry in this garden.

The plan was beautiful, so were the trees and shrubs. They grew to fill their allotted spaces. I grew too, and sat in a cane chair in the shade of the weeping apple tree memorising Shakespeare's sonnets for end-of-year exams, which came in hot December: 'Shall I compare thee to a summer's day? . . .' All around me was peaceful spreading space, hot sun on grass and dappled shadow, but not many flowers. The flowers did not *do*. The wisteria wreathed the fat stuccoed pillars of the verandahs but never flowered, nor did the paeony at its feet. The lily-of-the-valley did not spread. My mother mourned the fact, and blamed the roots of the towering Lombardy poplars that grew down one side of the first garden. She was English and grieved over her so-called herbaceous border, which never matched her memories of borders in English gardens, though every summer the moment came when a *Lilium regale* (we called it a Christmas lily) flowered, and so did a delphinium.

Every summer, the Christmas lily fell victim to the secateurs and came inside. Having given up hope of floral displays in the garden, we picked our best flowers for the house. As I grew older, I was allowed to 'do the flowers', particularly a leafy mixed bunch, overcrowded in a tall, trumpet-shaped crystal vase which stood in the drawing room on the baby grand piano. You picked the flowers in the early morning, before the sun was strong. You stripped all the lower leaves from the stems and gave the flowers a long drink in a big white china pail. If you had picked any Iceland poppies – they grew like weeds in Melbourne gardens and I thought them very common – you had to burn the cut tips of their hairy stems in the lighted gas-ring; the smell was acrid, the sap hissed. You started your arrangement by putting large sprays of flowering shrubs round the back and fanning out at each side, then you stuck your choicer blooms one by one into the middle. Sometimes they settled down and complemented each other, more often they didn't quite; but my mother encouraged me and always said the flowers looked very nice.

She was modest, gentle and undemanding. She would do simple jobs of upkeep, watering and dead-heading in the garden, but the mysteries of cultivation she assumed must be left to paid employees. She also assumed that our garden would never flower well. It did not occur to her that she herself could be a gardener. She recognised and respected the category, however. Often she would say, with admiring wistfulness, of friends, 'She's a great gardener . . .'. This meant that the friends filled their hours doing mysterious things deep in the borders, harmless, bewildering, boring and therefore rather pitiable. Why weren't they using their brains? I thought. Perhaps they were atrophied. I did not know that gardening is emotional, yet soothing. It fills a need, and restores a faith.

My mother walked round other people's gardens, exclaiming at their beauty, and repeating rapturously the names of roses, like talismans. These roses festooned the pergolas and trellises of privileged Melbourne gardens in a suburb called Toorak: 'Mme Butterfly', shell pink and scented, the swoony crimson climber 'Château de Clos Jouveaux', and the fashionable pink and gold 'Shot Silk', echoing the effect of the shot silk cushion covers of the day. The pergolas were there to divide these big suburban gardens into compartments. There was no shortage of land; no one was yet clamouring to carve up big gardens and build new houses on them. And so, over an acre or more, the gardens spread themselves; shallow steps led down to sunken gardens, there were wild gardens, formal gardens with lily ponds edged with paving and, behind heavily creepered netting beyond the rose gardens, lawn tennis courts with little pavilions beside them to keep the sun off resting players. The turquoise-blue swimming pools, today seen from the air in a pattern of parallelograms, had not yet arrived.

I, too, admired and envied these other people's gardens in Toorak. They were an evocation of Edwardian England living on in the thirties of the southern hemisphere. They largely eschewed native flora, the eucalypts and tea-trees, which are now, at last, so fashionable. They did admit wattle (what the English call 'mimosa'), for wattle is, after all, Australia's national flower, and the soft canary yellow powder-puffs smell honey-sweet in spring. But they despised many other glamorous half-hardy plants: arum lilies were banished as coarse weeds; agapanthus, so big, so blue, so bold, were not much prized; canna lilies were regarded as fit only for vulgar municipal displays; cinerarias were hackneyed stop-gaps, pelargoniums and geraniums beneath contempt. The very phrase 'half-hardy' had no meaning, for almost every desirable garden plant was hardy here, and the word 'hardy' itself was used to mean, not frost-proof, but fool-proof. There were no greenhouses in those gardens and no cold frames. Pale blue plumbago spread in the shrubberies; purple bougainvillea wreathed verandah posts with its papery triangular flowers, and there was no problem in getting the orange trumpets of the campsis or bignonia to open on a wall. Oleanders flowered in big tubs; pittosporum hedges were a commonplace with their neat and shiny leaves the colour of pea soup and their vanilla-scented flowers. There was a vast evergreen called a 'Moreton Bay fig' which spread in some old gardens. But traditional 'English trees' (meaning deciduous trees), 'English flowers' and 'English lawns' remained the things to go for. And so the hoses played all summer long; yards of rubber hose-pipe fed galvanised iron pipes with three jets in them, designed to water a whole length of border at a time. When the hot north wind blew, you stayed indoors with the windows shut, but in the evening and early morning you turned on all the garden taps. Even so, most lawns were threatened with dead patches, and the grass itself was often coarse and not a particularly vivid green.

But then there was the light – the brilliantly clear, sharp Australian light which marked off these gardens for ever from their English ancestors; everything was in focus, there were no blurred edges, no pastel shadings. The birds, too, were vivid and decidedly un-English. The wrens had breasts of cerulean blue; rosella parrots in gaudy red and blue or emerald green stripped fruit from ornamental trees; and in the evenings dark fell suddenly and mosquitoes whined and cicadas clicked.

In winter the watering ceased but the flowering continued. Heavily scented daphne (*Daphne odora*) was a commonplace, and people cut sprigs of it to wear in their lapels. Florists sold shoulder sprays of another heavily scented flower, boronia, which was like chocolate-brown lily-of-the-valley, each little bell lined with yellow. Vases were full of *Iris stylosa*; short narcissi bloomed and so did primroses, and an almond tree beside our front gate broke into celestial pink against the clear blue winter sky. There was even a climbing pink rose called 'Lorraine Lee' which flowered in winter. It was hard to detect where winter ceased and spring began.

When summer came again, trees flowered irrepressibly over every fence and along every suburban street. Jacaranda trees burst, in December, into improbable showers of intense wisteria-mauve. A little later, towering free-standing specimens of *Magnolia grandiflora* carried scented parchment chalices 25cm (10in) across. There was an odd tree that we called a 'pepper tree' (*Schinus molle*), which challenged children to climb it, being low-branching, tall and strong; its leaves were ferny, soft green, and it had clusters of shiny little peppers in sweet, cool pink. A young English milliner who came to stay with us collected bunches of the peppers, intending to take them back to London and attach them to the brims of hats. But within a week they wrinkled, lost their sheen, and dropped.

The small, square, front gardens of one-storey villas in the older suburbs of Melbourne were often planted with a palm tree in the middle of a front lawn of buffalo grass. These palms had plump trunks like pineapples, and the palm fronds fanned out wide, half-hiding the iron-lace verandahs behind them. I learnt to abhor the palms and laugh at the iron-lace. The modern outer suburbs had one-storey stucco houses with twisty pillars and Spanish-style tiles, and standard roses along the front path.

In such a suburb lived the one devoted gardener in our family, Uncle George. Retired, bent double, living on a modest pension, he had a small bungalow with a flat rectangular garden behind it, enclosed by wooden fences. As in our original garden, so here there was no sense of privacy, there were no subdivisions, no invitation to the visitor to explore. It offered the mixture as

before: a concrete path down the middle and borders along all
the fences. But, because he loved to grow things, he had borders
along both sides of the central path too. The tedium of visits
to Uncle George's garden lingers in my mind. My mother went
round the garden with him; I trailed behind. They stopped at
each shrub in turn. Uncle George pointed, and introduced it;
my mother pointed, and nodded, and asked questions. As the
years went by, Uncle George's lawns filled up. He was fitting
in more plants, each in its small island bed – the lawn was
peppered with them. The thing was the suburban equivalent
of an orchard. All that mattered was fostering new shrubs, and
the more difficult they were to acclimatise the more absorbing
they were. He grew a gardenia with petals like white kid and
a scent of sheer romance. But the total garden picture meant
nothing to him.

Our garden was all design and no plantsmanship. Uncle
George's was all plantsmanship and no design. I assumed
that plantsmanship was gardening and design was something
else, and I knew I was dead bored with gardening. I did not
like, or believe in, the small rectangle of soil on which I was
encouraged, as a child, to sow nasturtium seeds. The seeds were
too big to be convincing, and even rather hurtful to the feelings,
like over-large print in a child's first reader. I dreaded the yearly
chore of squatting by the primroses in spring and picking every
flower so that more would come. Just as bad, in a different
way, was the chore of the lavender: stripping the grey husks
of flowers from the dry stems on to a sheet of newspaper, to
await being stitched into mauve organdie lavender bags. When
I grew up, I did not readily volunteer to hose the fuchsias and
hydrangeas in the front garden on hot summer nights. I did not
dream of gardening myself until I came to England.

And it was twenty years before I understood that Uncle
George's garden and our Edna Walling garden were the two
poles on which the whole world of gardening turns.

II

In a London Terrace

Our England is a garden, and such gardens are not made
By singing: 'Oh, how beautiful!' and sitting in the shade.

Rudyard Kipling, 'The Glory of the Garden'

I was married and lived at the top of a narrow London
house, looking down upon the gardens far below. There were
two old cherry trees with a froth of white blossom in spring,
followed by real, dark cherries for the birds to eat. There
were slightly undulating garden walls, made of London stock
brick, darkened with age, where toadflax grew from the mortar.
Ancient pear trees towered in our neighbours' gardens to left
and right; there had once been a pear orchard here, they said,
before the houses came. You could lean out and look along the
backs of the terraced houses and see in spring the serried
ranks of blossoming trees in white and pink and crab-apple
red, and guess at the unseen gardens below the walls. The backs
of old London terraces follow a regular pattern, with sash
windows staggered – one up, one down; often, there were
later additions, bathrooms with new downpipes. The gardens
were long and narrow – 'cat-runs', people called them – of
varying length, twenty-seven of them in all, side by side; and,
indeed, two handsome ginger cats stepped delicately along our
walls each day. We were at one end, the end where the gardens
were shortest. They got longer as they went up the gentle slope,
from number one to number twenty-seven. In some, the soil level

was higher than in others, so they seemed to have lower walls, and some were very narrow indeed. The one in the middle was twice as wide as any other, to match its house. Ours was 27m (90 ft) long and 5m (17 ft) wide.

It was Eileen's (my mother-in-law's) garden. She bought the run-down house in 1951 when house prices were depressed by the Korean war. It had belonged to a wrought-iron worker and heavy iron bolts and bars kept it safe from the outside world; growing out of the railings by the front steps was a black iron sunflower, lovingly wrought, like a flower from a William Morris wallpaper. The sunny front garden was on two levels with an old brick retaining wall between them. The back garden was shaded by the tall terraced houses and by the cherry trees, and had an Anderson air-raid shelter in the middle. Against the walls were two dark, dusty rhododendrons, the yellow rose 'Emily Gray' with a disappointing rambler scent, another yellow rambler with no scent at all, a gawky old moss rose leaning slightly forward on a single stem like the neck of a giraffe, and a slowly dying laburnum. 'Be careful of the laburnum', said Eileen. Someone had told her it was poisonous.

She was scribbling pencil sketches of how the garden should go. Fussiness was out: simplicity was the thing to aim at. She thought it should be mainly uninterrupted lawn; if the lawn were interrupted by beds or paths it would take too long to mow. The path should therefore go along one edge of it, and there should be straight, narrow borders round all the walls with a slightly deeper border at the far end where the sun touched for longest. In front of this border should be a square of paving for sitting on. The paving would have to be crazy, because you could get bits of broken York stone cheaply from the council; unbroken York slabs were too expensive. When she showed me her sketch I felt a vague unease. It took its orders from the long brick rectangle of the walls, and proposed no diversions, no variation on that theme.

'Could you perhaps break the left-hand border halfway along

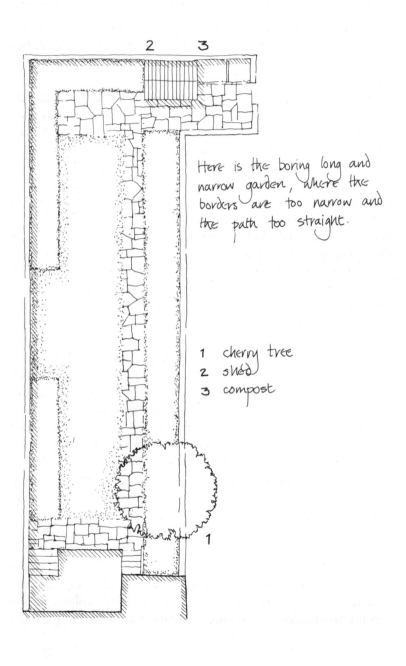

2   3

Here is the boring long and
narrow garden, where the
borders are too narrow and
the path too straight.

1 cherry tree
2 shed
3 compost

for a yard or two, and carry the grass right up to the wall there?
Just to vary things a bit?' I asked. She looked unconvinced, but
said 'OK,' because she didn't mind very much one way or the
other and wanted to be nice to me.

The first thing was to get rid of the air-raid shelter.
Beside it was a large mound of excavated yellow London clay.
Her sons set to work putting as much clay as they could back
into the hole made by the shelter, and spreading the rest over
the future lawn, a miserable inch or two of top-soil preserved
for surfacing. Then one of them laid the path. Laying crazy
paving is a tricky business, for the bits of stone come in
different thicknesses, so need to be sunk at different depths.
With patience and skill he got it reasonably level, and made
the jigsaw pattern of the stones reasonably tight, though there
was still plenty of room for future dandelions and grass to grow
between. The finished path looked uncompromisingly straight,
following its narrow course from the back steps straight down
the whole length of the garden to the bottom without a single
hesitation or momentary change of material or width. At the
far end, the garden took a turn; it was like a long leg with a
small foot attached. Turn the heel, and there was a little hidden
passage of trodden earth with a back gate and two rubbish bins.
It was to this rather banal finale that the path led.

Then came the making of the lawn. There was much
spiking of the surface area with a garden fork in the hope
of draining the clay, much levelling and raking, a bit of
fertilising, and then, in early April, they sowed grass seed
– a mixture with rye grass in it, said to be a wise choice
for difficult sites. They shook the seed conscientiously out of
a sieve after first dousing it in paraffin to keep off the birds.
They watched their bare seed-bed of soil through the kitchen
window. The seed was more visible than they thought it ought
to be, and looked dry, if not dead. Then one morning, about a
fortnight after the sowing, they saw the first little colony of thin
green grass blades all growing as straight as soldiers in a slight

hollow. 'It's germinating!' they cried, incredulous. 'It's begun!' It went on, but not everywhere. There were bare patches near the house, where the clay was stickiest, the shade densest. This became the 'lawn' down to which I looked at the end of their first year's gardening.

It was winter. All the back gardens were damply dark brown with untidy dead straw-coloured stems on top. Then came crocuses. I had not yet learnt to despise the fat Dutch hybrids in royal purple, gold and striped mauve and white; I marvelled at them. I had never seen a crocus in Australia. Then came daffodils, then sheets of bluebells – I had no idea that they could be regarded as invasive weeds. Happy though it is to grow up in a city where gardens flower all the year round, it is a different and thrilling happiness to live through dramatically changing seasons where winter is bare and the legend of Proserpina returning from the underworld is demonstrated to be true each spring.

Marvellous unknown things burst into bloom in May in our neighbours' gardens. There were clumps of showy, lavender-blue flowers along a path. Later came astonishing sturdy clumps of purple heads whose bells pointed up, not down. A low shrub of dazzling chalk white made a plump mound over a retaining wall. Further along this wall, an exquisite little weeping shrub burst into pea-flowers of cowslip colour. Delicate blue irises on slender stems shot up at the foot of the wall. I did not learn the names till later. (They were, in order, cranesbill, *Campanula glomerata*, perennial candytuft, *Cytisus x kewensis* and *Iris sibirica*.)

In the municipal flowerbeds in front of our terrace, the brilliant tulips flowered. I had never seen a tulip in Australia, either. Eileen, also Australian, had been inspired by great beds of tulips in a London park, a gift from the Netherlands after the war, and she had determined to make a joyous display of tulips in her own front garden. She arranged them formally, in a double row round a square of paving. The bulbs, fresh from de Jager's expert care, were satin-smooth and plump, with glimpses of cream showing through slits in their rich brown coats. In November she'd planted them, 23cm (9 in) apart, the tall white 'Zwanenburg' at the back, the yellow 'Niphetos' in the front. In the middle of the paving was a small square bed which she filled with cherry-red tulips. In spring the unpromising limp tulip leaves broke through the earth, then each plant produced its pointed bud on a strong but slender stem. The whole planting became a *tour de force*. Tall Darwin tulips are formal flowers, and the eye ran round their soldierly ranks rejoicing in the miracle that they were all present and correct, all flowering. But after three triumphant weeks their petals blew away, one by one, and gradually the leaves died down. Bluebells mysteriously appeared among them, spreading with robust confidence. Someone told Eileen she should lift the tulip bulbs and examine them for wireworm. A depressing ritual followed in which the bulbs, now dirty, subdividing or shrinking, were scrutinised. Most were judged to be defective. The only solution seemed to be to order new bulbs for next year. Meanwhile, nothing further happened in our front garden for the rest of the summer, and the chickweed spread.

But the back garden bloomed. Eileen had planted two lupins, a deep pink and a violet, and two delphiniums, one classic delphinium-blue, the other tinged with mauve. She had put a 'Crimson Glory' climbing hybrid tea rose against a wall. When the sun shone in June and July, she carried a tea-tray down the path and we all sat on the crazy paving and felt pleased with the garden's existence. The two delphiniums towered, fatly tapering and beautiful, in the border behind us; 'Crimson Glory' carried a few deeply desirable scented flowers. It was not too hot. The light was hazy, flattering. The soft bloom of an English garden was coming within reach.

Eileen belonged to the big band of garden owners who love flowers, know which ones they love best, plant some of these, then get on with their own lives and hope the plants will get on with theirs. Not for her were the excruciatingly prolonged games of choice with which obsessive gardeners while away the time: what will look best here – what should I plant there – which roses do I like best of all – what sort of picture should my garden make? Since this was long before the days of container plants in garden centres, she was denied the stimulus of instant gardening which she would have much enjoyed, and obliged to think ahead. Someone had recommended to her the famous old nursery firm, Jackman's of Woking, and she sat down with their catalogue and had a pleasant time leafing through it and concocting her list. She ordered a white lilac ('Nicer than purple, don't you think?'), a double philadephus which sounded more fun than the singles but turned out to be scentless, a semi-evergreen honeysuckle which turned out not to flower, *Clematis montana* which turned out to be too rampant for its allotted space, and a little crab apple which died. She also ordered her very favourite shrub, an apricot azalea, which she planted in a sunny corner of the front garden.

She knew something should be done about the sour, tired old soil. She sprinkled lime over it, and organised us with compost buckets in our kitchens which we emptied, when they became unbearably full, on to a rubbish dump called 'the compost heap' which took its place beside the dustbins round the corner at the bottom of the garden.

She had enthusiastic gardening friends who gave her things for her new garden out of their own gardens, and she gladly stuck them in: lily-of-the-valley in deep shade by the back door, bits of soft *Dicentra eximia*, London pride with its dull leathery rosettes of leaves edging the path further along, a few untidy bits of bergenia flapping their elephants' ears in the shade below some twiggy and shapeless hydrangeas with pink flowers, some bits of border phlox, a rooted cutting of winter jasmine, sweet-scented single pinks edging the sunny border near the delphiniums, purple flag irises behind the tulips in front, and surprising clumps of spiderwort coming up among rank grass by the front path along with leggy bits of lavender. An elderly friend arrived with a bare wand in her hand which she stuck into the far end of the shady border saying: 'It'll grow.' Nobody believed her, but it did. It was forsythia. There were also some untidy scraps of kerria here and there in double egg-yolk yellow.

Eileen loved her London garden, but her thoughts did not dwell on it for long. She was optimistic, impatient, warmly responsive to beauty but prepared to shrug her shoulders, laugh and look the other way when August came and there was nothing flowering in the garden. With August came a sense that the party was over, that there was no further party to look forward to. The freshness had gone out of that thrilling English leaf-green. A few attenuated hardy annuals, bits of clarkia and candytuft (reminders that in hopeful spring Eileen had been cheerfully scattering packets of seed) held mauve or pink heads about encroaching weeds. Brave self-seeded hollyhocks stood against walls among the dead seed-heads of foxgloves (also self-sown from next door), but their random red flowers were totally outnumbered by the lines of green buttons which marked the spots on the stem where earlier flowers had been. The phlox flowered a bit, but was no substitute for the lupins and delphiniums, and the pink hydrangeas beneath the cherry tree did little to lift the heart – to lift my heart in those days they would have needed to be bright blue. It was almost a relief when winter came and there was nothing more to be disappointed about, for we expected nothing of the winter garden.

Before the following spring, Eileen had remarried and re-turned to Australia, where she began enthusiastically to plant the now-favoured native wattles and eucalypts in a sandy seaside soil. With characteristic and overwhelming generosity, she gave her London house to us. And it became clear that if anyone was to tend this blithely started English garden, it was me.

III

Learning to Garden

And some can pot begonias and some can bud a rose,
And some are hardly fit to trust with anything that grows . . .

Rudyard Kipling, 'The Glory of the Garden'

My neighbour looked over the wall and offered me a ticket to the Chelsea Flower Show, and so, for the first time, I passed up and down those scented, one-way aisles in the great marquee, shuffling along with the crowds on the fast-balding grass between the white ropes, and stared, and read names, and noted what I liked on a piece of paper, and collected catalogues and leaflets. I made two discoveries: begonias and miniature roses. The begonias on Blackmore and Langdon's stand took my breath away. Such impossible glamour! I had never heard of them before. Size, texture, colour – surely I could never grow such things? But the man in charge thought I could, so, after much hesitation and comparison of yellow with white and flame, I ordered one, a double salmon pink, at least 10cm (4 in) across. The rose catalogue I took home, and filled in my order for a 'Miniature Rose Collection' – six bush and two standard.

They arrived in a box, more thrilling than a dress box, packed with exquisite care, smelling of moisture and of life. Two of them were called 'Sweet Fairy', and were scented double pink. There was a narrow border at the top of the retaining wall in the front garden which I considered to be an ideal place for them: the right aspect, the right size. I dug a trowel into the grey and stony earth and in they went in a row: two bush, one standard, two bush, one standard, two bush. The standards had come complete with their own little green stakes. They did not die – they flowered, and I was captivated.

'Look what I got at the Chelsea Show!' I said in gratitude to my neighbour, proud of my unusual and tasteful find.

Then a dozen potted begonias arrived – it turned out you couldn't order just one; I had misunderstood. I wasn't quite so pleased with myself, but a book from the library explained how to cultivate them. I copied it all out into an exercise book. It said: 'Starting the tubers yourself is a very simple matter, especially as they do not require full sunshine . . . any fairly light space in a room where the atmosphere is not too dry will answer . . .'. We had a small sunless room which would become a baby's room when we had a baby. Meanwhile, it became the Begonia Room. The first dozen were already in leaf, each in its own small pot. As they grew, we transplanted them into larger pots which we bought for the purpose along with moss peat, following the book's advice. We stood them round in the shade at the top of the basement area steps. They flowered, but did little for the general appearance of the garden. Their subsequent history, overwintering in the Begonia Room, was not particularly successful.

But now I began to borrow other books from our local public library. Gradually I worked my way along the gardening shelves, making notes of the writers' recommendations in my begonia exercise book – plants, not methods, were what I noted. The names were all new to me, but if the writer was persuasive and the descriptions tempted, down they went: cynoglossum, potentilla, dodecatheon, geum, *Anthericum liliago*, hemerocallis, *Tiarella cordifolia*, auricula, hellebore. These outlandish names were spoken only within the secret society of gardeners, and it seemed unlikely that I would ever memorise them or ensnare many of them for our garden, but at least they were safely in my book.

Our neighbours were busy people, but every now and then, on sunny weekend mornings, they would emerge through their back doors and start 'doing the garden'. How did they know what to do? They relied a good deal on secateurs, cutting things down and bundling up what they recognised as garden rubbish. I, too, had secateurs, a cheap, blunt, silver-coloured left-behind pair of Eileen's. But I simply could not spot what should be cut. I did, however, recognise the more obvious weeds: grass, chickweed, and dandelions. And though I had never heard of bittercress or enchanter's nightshade, I assumed that the pervasive, tiny thing with ferny leaves and the taller thing with horizontal white roots must be weeds as well. I began to pull them out with my hands, leaving the roots behind, then got a rather stiff pair of gardening gloves. Then someone told me that the hoe is the thing to use for weeding. We had a hoe but I found it very awkward, jabbing and pushing and then perhaps scooping and raking, and I did not know whether to leave the weeds lying on the surface to rot down or whether to rake them up. I settled for a compromise. One day when I was jabbing away with my hoe, my extra-talented gardening neighbour from the right-hand side looked over the wall and said: 'Ah, that's what *I* should be doing.' It was a moment of pride, a milestone in my gardening life.

Weeding was boring at the time but rewarding afterwards, infinitely more rewarding than housework. You vacuum a carpet, the crumbs are gone but the carpet looks otherwise just as before. You weed a flower border and there is dramatic metamorphosis: the plants stand out, the soil looks nice, the texture changes, the colour changes, the smell changes. On sunny days I too came through the back door to 'do the garden'.

I had read about chamomile lawns and thought it would be a clever dodge to sow chamomile seed in the chinks of crazy paving where at present grass grew strongly and had to be scraped out. The chamomile would never need cutting, it would spread and leave no room for grass and smell delicious underfoot. But I must have got the wrong seed: it did not spread, it grew upwards, taller than grass and more untidy. The idea languished.

I now discovered that bluebells could be regarded as weeds and that they were threatening to take over our front garden altogether. I began to hate them, and dug my cheap trowel down into the hard earth to eradicate them. Up came inches of white stem, but where was the bulb? Broken off deep down – the sneak – and left behind.

I knew our garden was full of gaps, and that in order to fill these wisely I should learn to recognise a few more plants. We caught the train that loops round North London from Broad Street to Richmond and got off at Kew Gardens in the spring. A short walk down a straight wide road with appropriately fertile, tended and mature private gardens on either side, through the handsome wrought-iron gates, and there we were, on the huge lawns, free to wander at will over the grass and beneath the magnificent specimen trees. We reached the rhododendron banks and gasped at the towering walls of frilly pinks and whites and reds. The two dirty old rhododendrons still survived at home, but we determined to do better. When Jackman's catalogue arrived, unexpected but warmly welcomed, later that year, we ordered a rich crimson rhododendron called 'Britannia'. Its description, compact and hardy, seemed to fit our bill, and I thought intense colours would lift our garden scene.

I went back to Kew Gardens later, by myself, and found the iris garden. The ravishing individual creatures were arranged in blocks of colour, their fans of leaves so stiff, their stems

PLATE 1   *A front garden in Grove Terrace, brimful of sun-loving, aromatic flowers.*

so straight and smooth and strong, their flowers of such exquisite fragility with bearded petals falling and other curved petals rising in a cup round a scented throat. D.H. Lawrence described the perfume of irises as 'raw and coarse', 'brutal' and 'sickening', but it is also sweet. Of all the colour combinations I saw that day the one I liked best was a trio of blue, yellow and velvet brown: 'Great Lakes', 'Fair Elaine' and 'Stained Glass'. I had brought my exercise book; I took down their names. I was beginning serious plans for our garden.

I planned to have a bed of irises behind the edging of pinks in the sunny corner of the back garden. I planned to fill all the blank and boring spaces of the borders with eye-catching flowers. In particular, there should be a rose bed in the front garden on the higher level, in front of the area railings and opposite the strip of miniature roses, to carry the show on when the tulips were over. The damp old brick walls should carry climbing plants as well. There was no hurry. It was important to make sound choices, and fun to postpone decisions.

Gardening had now revealed itself to me, not as exhausting drudgery or finicky skill, but as concerned with choice, like shopping. You decided what you needed, you searched for things you liked and, if you could, you bought them. It was more fun than shopping for food or clothes and, in those days, cheaper. It was not unlike decorating a room or rearranging furniture. The whole thing was governed by visual taste, but instead of sewing or painting, or pushing furniture about, you got hold of a spade or trowel and dug a hole in the earth and put your plant into it and tucked it up with earth again, and then you watered it. It was more deeply satisfying than interior decoration because it was life you were dealing with, and it

PLATE 2 *Patterned plants round a pillar set off each other's statuesque profiles in a Richmond garden.*

turned out that the things you planted had a great will to live, despite the lacklustre London soil which smelt sooty and sour and was full of stones and cat-messes.

Our sunniest wall was at the end of the garden and I had to choose for it something worthy, something which throve in warmth. I discovered what it was to be at Kew, on a winter's morning. In January I rediscovered it in a doctor's waiting room where a big jug was filled with bare brown twigs to which clung starched little cowslip-yellow bells, scenting the air with vanilla sweetness. It was *Chimonanthus praecox*, the winter sweet. In summer its fresh green leaves make it resemble a fan-trained cherry against a wall – a nice background for summer flowers. In winter its flowers break from the joints of the bare twigs, translucent downward-pointing bells with an outer circle of tapered yellow sepals and a distinct inner circle of smaller petals, sometimes purplish, sometimes (as in the variety *C. praecox* 'Luteus') primrose. Many books had urged me to plant for winter in a town garden, and sometimes it seemed that there were as many enthusiasts for winter gardening as for all the other seasons of the year. And all these fans of winter flowers praised the winter sweet; they assured their readers that it would grow 3m (10 ft) high and 2.5m (8ft) wide, given a sunny spot, and that it would bear an abundance of winter flowers. Clearly that was what happened to the shrub whose branches found their way into the doctor's waiting room, for who would slash lavish branches from a precious shrub and carry them to work unless they had branches to spare?

I never had branches to spare. The most I achieved was a couple of twigs in a sherry glass, with a couple of flowers apiece. Yet even four flowers could scent the room. It was tantalising: a good choice gone wrong, and I did not know why.

Kew supplied other dubious inspirations. In midsummer I saw a rose I had loved as a child in a friend's mother's Melbourne garden: 'Cécile Brunner', a real miniature, looking as if it was moulded out of porcelain to go on the lid of a

Dresden china powder bowl. My friend's mother picked tight nosegays of it, and it had the fascination of all miniatures: how could something so small be so faithful a reproduction of the real thing? For 'Cécile Brunner' was like a perfect hybrid tea – 'Madame Butterfly' or 'Lady Sylvia' writ small – many times lovelier than my rather shapeless miniatures in the front garden, but produced on a much larger plant. The plant I saw at Kew was large indeed: it was the climbing form of 'Cécile Brunner', luxuriating on a rose arch over a path. I thought I would send it up the front of our house, where it would get plenty of sun and remind me of my friend's mother's garden, and I, too, would pick tight perfumed nosegays when it flowered.

I did. For the rose raced 3.5cm (12ft) upwards beside the front door and 5.5m (18ft) along the wrought-iron balcony which it threatened to pull down, and it flung long wands out west and south towards our neighbours' balconies and out over our front garden. Pruning these wands was a nightmare but, for a brief fortnight in June, before the petals fell and turned brown on the frontpath, it looked a picture.

'Isn't the rose a picture!' came the soft voice of an Irish tenant of ours one sunny day. He was not looking at 'Cécile Brunner', but at the undistinguished yellow rambler which had survived from an earlier era in the back garden. I acquiesced, but disagreed in my mind. I did not know the name of this rose, but knew I could do better. Its flowers were small and rather weedy-looking, I thought. I also knew that, particularly in a small garden, you should tolerate nothing but the best.

So one day, with prodigious, back-breaking effort, I dug out the yellow rambler. I had no idea how deep the roots of an elderly rose will go. I replaced it with 'Nevada', the modern shrub rose which has been praised prodigiously from the moment of its breeding. It is a glorious plant; its branches spread out and bow down to the tips with their load of large and loose cream flowers interspersed with neatly tapered golden buds. Sometimes, in a wet summer, it aspires to be pink. Mine had to grow in shade, but might not have minded that; I have seen it grow amongst a crowd of other shrubs in a shaded front garden where it shoots high and pretends to be a climber. But I did not know, when I planted it in the old rambler's bed, that there is such a thing as 'rose sickness'. You should not plant a rose where another rose has grown unless you change the top-soil first. My 'Nevada' flowered a little, but failed to prosper.

'Blanc Double de Coubert', the hybrid rugosa, was more successful, growing in the front garden where no rose had been before. It, too, was an inspiration from Kew, where I first met it growing as a free-standing shrub in grass. It had carrying-power: I saw it from a distance across the lawn and wondered what it could be: I did not realise that this rather coarse, bright green shrub was a rose at all. 'Flowers like lovely frilly white camellias', I noted in my exercise book. But when I bent over them, they smelt divinely rose-like.

You cannot go on indefinitely with the delightful hobby of reading about plants, inspecting them, choosing them, buying them and planting them. My conscience mumbled that I should embark, periodically, on wearisome horticultural tasks designed to make the plants grow better. First there was the question of the London soil. My library books had talked about soil, and the feeding of it, and how you should not put on lime and bonemeal at the same time. Some of them seemed pretty sniffy about lime itself, and spoke of how gardeners in the past ruined their kitchen gardens by over-liming. I began to go off the lime idea, particularly round the two sooty rhododendrons, but decided to sprinkle bonemeal in the autumn and grimly spread the 'compost' as a mulch in spring. No one had told me how much better it would be to scatter a dressing of balanced fertiliser like Growmore first.

I did not really believe that our compost was any good. By the time I spread it the kitchen waste had entirely disappeared but the garden rubbish had not. The stuff I spread was all little twigs and half-decayed leaves and smelt rather less promising than the soil itself. I did not realise that you should chop up the long or tough things before you put them on the heap. I did not know that dry material should be watered. I never used an activator. But I did follow a terrible gardening ordeal called 'turning the compost'. When I had spread one season's heap over the beds, I transferred a second heap, which was waiting beside it in a makeshift cage, into its place. It was fun at first, putting the unsightly kitchen refuse out of sight. The bright colours of orange peel and banana skins and egg shell would quickly disappear below slimy browns, and soon you would come to bright pink worms. But as you got further down the pile, lunging in and forking out became annoyingly strenuous; it was hard to know which tool was least bad: the big old fork, off which half the load would drop each time you lifted it, or the rusty shovel, which was difficult to load up in the first place.

For one brief period someone who lived halfway up the terrace gave over their long narrow garden to a horse, which used to walk in and out through their Georgian front door and down their hall passage. They sold horse manure by the sack; these were happy days for terrace gardeners. Our compost, mixed with straw and dung, briefly seemed better.

Spreading the compost, and turning the compost, only occupied one desperate day a year. I concocted other conscience-soothing garden jobs attached to different seasons. The compost ritual occurred in spring. So did feeding the lawn. Every April, half the lawn seemed bald – no grass, just damp mossy earth – and every April I bought a large and expensive carton of combined weedkiller and lawn fertiliser and sprinkled it carefully all over the grass and bare earth alike. If it rained, not immediately but two or three days later as the instructions on the packet required, the technique worked and a sort of lawn appeared. Later I worked over the lawn, snipping off the strong whiskers of rye grass that rose high above the general level. In summer

I weeded and hoed; I divided the irises, forking out the layers of knobbly tubers in trefoil fans like crows' feet; I broke off bits and replanted them precariously on the surface of the bed as all the experts advised, just covering their sparse roots with earth; then, miserable at the waste but obedient to the book, I threw the rest on to the latest compost heap.

I also washed the filthy leaves of the rhododendrons (this was still the era of coal fires). Each one was sponged with warm water and detergent, and they gave their thanks in a multiplication of buds next spring. 'Look! The rhododendrons are turning pink!' I cried, for cochineal pink, like tissue paper, was peeping through between the green blades of the buds, one in each rosette of leathery leaves. It was a delusion: the flowers opened white as before. Our new crimson rhododendron never flowered much, but the spring-cleaned white ones prospered. I moved the little sunset-apricot azalea away from Eileen's original, mistaken placing of it, for I had read about aspects as well as soils, and knew that certain plants need sun and others shade. Sun was a precious rarity in our London garden, and nothing was to be allowed to have it that could do without it. Curiously, the azalea did not flower as well in its new, shady place as it did in its old, sunny one, but at least I discovered the possibility of moving plants about.

In the autumn I swept up the leaves with a beautiful new rubber rake; I piled them high in the borders, following the suspiciously easy advice of Michael Haworth Booth in his book *Effective Flowering Shrubs* (Collins, 1951).

All this activity was spread over three years, or more. There was still no baby in our Begonia Room. For the time being, then, plants became my charges, my children. I joined the Royal Horticultural Society and every fortnight in the growing season I pushed through the turnstiles in Vincent Square under the porch where the bold notice ran: '*Today's Show Is In Both Halls*'.

Up the steps I went, to be wrapped round in the embalmed

spaces of this remarkable hall built in the 1930s, arched and vaulted like a latterday cathedral but with a clock, not an altar, at one end and a raised dais at the other, where gardeners sat in rows, as at a theatre, eating their packed lunches. It was a capsule, an insulated world removed from outside cares and longings, and filled with flower scents. The nurserymen's displays glimmered and beckoned like shrines, mounted on waist-high stands with green hessian to the floor and pyramids of plants above. Everything was labelled and everything could be ordered, though in those days nothing could be bought at the show itself. I worshipped at those shrines, and found a promise of fulfilment in the solitary quest for perfect flowers.

I moved from stand to stand, selecting and rejecting in my mind, collecting sixpenny lists of plants and annotating the margins. My tastes in flowers were changing. The new Spirit of the Age had got hold of me, turning me from the large and bright and double towards the small and pale and single. At the early spring show, bewitching tiny bulbs appeared to grow out of mounds of moss or beech leaves or rich brown peat. They were miniature narcissi, muscari, tiny irises barely 15cm (6in) high. I found an anemone quite unlike the ones with fringed black stamens in purple and scarlet bunches sold from barrows at street corners. It was a long-stemmed anemone of palest creamy green, and I hugged myself in recognition that this was a flower I must have.

In late April I raced through the doors, ignoring the towering displays of giant daffodils, golden, white and pink. The little auriculas and primulas looked like embroidery on a dark velvet ground. I saw a fritillary, *Fritillaria meleagris*, for the first time. I had only read about them in Matthew Arnold's 'The Scholar-Gipsy':

> I know what white, what purple fritillaries
> The grassy harvest of the river-fields
> Above by Ensham, down by Sandford, yields . . .

White, purple . . . clear and bold, they sounded. I did not dream that they were chequered like a snake's skin, small clean-cut bells with pointed edges. I ordered six.

At a May show I saw a miraculous sight. It was a poppy, and it was not orange but butterfly blue, the blue of lapis lazuli: meconopsis. With bated breath, I ordered three.

In June I found a stall full of little grey and silver shrubs and garden pinks. I lingered while an elderly lady in a wide red hat discussed with another elderly lady how her last year's purchases had done. 'Oh, my "Doris" did well,' she said. 'Of course, I adore "Doris", but much as I adore her, I do want something else.'

But I had to choose my roses. They were arranged, tier upon tier, in bowls and metal vases, dozens of identical, long-stemmed blooms stuck into damp Oasis and arranged to fan out into domes and cones. Hybrid teas and floribundas jostled for position; each grower had new named varieties to sell. One whole display was given over to the pinkest of the pinks, the tallest of the tall, the 'Queen Elizabeth' rose, and a tall man with wide moustaches stood beside it, accepting congratulations.

I chose old-favourite roses for my small front bed: 'Mme Butterfly', 'Comtesse Vandal', 'Violinista Costa' and 'Virgo' – archetypal shell-pink, apricot, flame and tight-furled white – to be delivered in November.

By August the mingled perfumes of phlox and buddleia in the Horticultural Halls brought a wave of sadness over me, and yet the autumn shows, with their mellow leaves and berries, their brimming plates of polished apples, cheered with unexpected warmth. And soon it was time for the early bulbs again.

My purchases did not prosper. The meconopsis made basal leaves, but failed to flower. The anemone disappeared. Only one fritillary established itself, and that a white one. The HT roses in the front bed never did much good, though I learnt to strip greenfly off the young stems between finger and thumb and gave them handfuls of rose fertiliser after doing my best to prune them. There was a rose here, a rose there – nice for picking, like the isolated blooms in the Melbourne garden of my childhood. If they had all flowered abundantly, how nice would my chosen mixed colours have looked? Not very.

At the end of five apprentice years, I was still not a skilful gardener. Impatience prevented my taking proper care. Clumsiness made me crush plants underfoot when stepping backwards out of a border. Stinginess prevented me from removing the semi-failures altogether: the unflowering honey-suckle, the boring forsythia, the scentless philadelphus should all have gone. But if you have been brought up to be frugal, it is very difficult to throw plants away. I did not water my plants enough. Indeed, since this was England, I found it hard to believe that they needed any watering at all; it wasn't hot enough for watering. I had got it into my head that 'chemicals' were bad, so I did not feed my plants enough either. I should have spread a general fertiliser all over the beds at the rate of 120 g per square metre (4 oz per square yard) every spring.

But something was more deeply wrong: it was the layout of the garden. That rectangle of grass, those narrow borders round the walls, that straight path of crazy paving, uncompromising in its refusal to change width or direction, added up to a predicta-bility as stifling to the imagination as that first strict Australian garden. Might a sundial, strategically placed, put things right? I could not think where to put one. I simply went on planting, and alongside failure eventually came success.

IV

Succeeding with Plants

First came a magnolia tree.

Only the most perverse can resist the glory of flowering magnolias in spring. The flowers are so big, so abundant, the little pale leaves still so sparse, the trees – if given elbow-room – so shapely, that passers-by must gasp at the massed goblets, pearl-white brushed at the base on the outside with rose, opening their rounded shapes in April sunshine. The passers-by tend to call them 'tulip trees'. Why not? That's what they look like: spreading oriental trees, with ranks of tulip flowers poised along the silver-grey branches, all pointing up towards the light. As the days go by, the flowers open wider, the sun seems to drain the rose-colour away, and finally the thick white petals begin to fall, lying soft and bruised on the soil below.

I decided we should put a magnolia in the middle of the formal tulip garden in front of our house. Abandon the scarlet tulips in the square central bed; put the magnolia there instead, and plant a square of magnolia-coloured tulips round it. (I was beginning to glimpse the possibilities of 'match' rather than 'mix' in garden planting.) I found such a tulip at a Chelsea flower show: 'Aristocrat', a tall Darwin tulip, white tipped with plum. This matching idea proved

The paved front garden has a magnolia on the lower
level surrounded by tulips and a hopeful row of
miniature roses above the retaining wall.

disappointing and muddling in practice, but the magnolia triumphed.

It was the usual *Magnolia x soulangeana*, not one of the more rarefied varieties. When it arrived I was in bed with 'flu, but I had been reading about its requirements and had already laid in a bag of peat, failing the recommended leaf mould. My brother-in-law, who shared the house with us, undertook the planting. I gave him a feverish lecture on how the job was to be done, by rote from my book-learning. A wide, deep hole was to be dug, two spits of soil were to be removed, there were to be layers of damp peat mixed with bonemeal, and a final mulch of peat on top. He did it all as he was bidden, translating theory into practice with no fuss. And the tree grew and flowered and spread for twenty years, its roots finding cool spaces under paving, starting to flower when it was barely a metre (3ft) high. There came a nightmare morning when workmen laying a new gas main dug a channel right across and through its roots. Panic-stricken by reports that the one thing magnolias resent is disturbance of their brittle roots, we phoned a tree surgeon, and followed his calm instructions: fill in the trench with peat and fertiliser. The magnolia showed no signs of the amputations that had happened below ground, and is still there today.

One's choices are flighty, inconsistent. I chose the magnolia from the evidence of my own eyes in spring. The fig, my second success with trees, I chose as a result of a colleague's chance remark which had lingered in my mind.

'I'd love a little London courtyard garden,' she said over morning coffee, 'with a *fig* tree!' Her eyes signalled to me that I must agree.

'Yes!' I agreed, and we both laughed with pleasure.

So when one of our ancient cherry trees died, we replaced it with a fig, though ours was not a courtyard garden. We planted it in a small raised semi-circular bed constructed with old London bricks against one of the boundary walls, for I had read that figs fruit best when their root space is restricted. But we did not spread concrete over the bottom of the bed, so the fig sent its eager roots down through the London clay and grew prodigiously, upwards, sideways, and fanning out across the garden, multistemmed. In summer, carrying its big lobed leaves, it divided the garden into two with a dense screen of scalloped green. You could not see through it to the sunny end when you emerged from the back door. I liked its leaves for thus bringing privacy to our garden, as they did to our First Parents at the Fall of Man. In winter, when the soft, spongy leaves fell, you could see right down the garden to the end wall again, and its taller branches made shadows on the brick. But there was such a complication of twisting, pigeon-grey branches, each curving upward like candelabra, that the time came when I had to prune out at least some superfluous branches, especially those that touched the ground. D.H. Lawrence has described the behaviour of the fig tree exactly. 'And let us notice it behave itself', he says, in a poem called 'Bare Fig-Trees':

> And watch it putting forth each time to heaven,
> Each time straight to heaven,
> With marvellous naked assurance each single twig,
> Each one setting off straight to the sky
> As if it were the leader, the main-stem, the forerunner,
> Intent to hold the candle of the sun upon its socket-tip,
> It alone.

Fig wood is soft and sappy, easy to cut through with long-handled secateurs, and when you burn your prunings, juices come bubbling out. A few small figs would hang on our tree all winter, but never ripened the following summer into edible fruits. Professional gardeners do not allow their fig trees to grow into exuberant tangles like this; they clip them against walls so that they look more like neat climbers than trees. There are two like that in Trafalgar Square, adding trim green to the grey façade of the National Gallery in summer. Our fig was called 'Brown Turkey', a memorably inappropriate name for this greenest of trees. It is its sheer leafiness and hint of Mediterranean sun that makes it life-enhancing in a city garden. But when the time came to sell that terrace house, thirty-five years on, the young son of our prospective purchasers pointed to the fig and said: 'We're going to have THAT out!'

Underneath the fig tree was spread a silver-mauve carpet of success: *Crocus tomasinianus*, starting as twelve tiny bulbs. I had now absorbed the idea that small species crocuses are more desirable than the fat Dutch hybrid crocus, and when these crocuses began to flower, and spread, I realised this was true. It is a fugitive beauty, dependent on the sun. In winter when the fig tree boughs were bare, there was an hour or two when the February sun might touch the ground below it, and the slender, silver buds of the 'tommy' crocuses would open into stars – massed lilac stars, a whole galaxy of radiant flowers to every bulb. Even if this miracle only happened once or twice each year, it was worthwhile. The sun came, the crocuses opened, the spectator caught the moment, and marvelled. Then, when the flowers were over, bent and bowed, the striped leaves grew, furnishing that bald bit of 'lawn' under the fig tree before the fig's leaves came. There are many other species crocuses, coloured cream or gold or striped with blue or bronze. I tried some of them and they sometimes flowered, but it was only *Crocus tomasinianus* that spread itself with liberal spirit from my original prim semicircle into an ever-widening sheet of flowers. In summer no one could even see this bare bit of grassless lawn under the dense fig tree, when the crocuses were dormant underground.

A third lucky choice of tree, or rather shrub, depended upon the written word. Michael Howarth Booth and Vita Sackville-West both spoke well of *Hoheria lyalli*: 'One of the most lovely of white-flowered deciduous shrubs ...' 'It really is a lovely thing ...'. I noted in my exercise book that it sounded right for us, flowering in July, a New Zealander liking a sheltered spot and not fussy about soil.

It arrived, it flourished, it grew 3m (10ft) tall. Its leaves were heart-shaped, pale green satin, seeming to borrow light from the incandescent clusters of cup-shaped flowers, each dangling a little on its slender stem and opening single with pale stamens, which burst into bloom just as the roses faded. It was more beautiful than mock orange except that it lacked a heady scent. The flowers and leaves together harmonised into a single airy lightness. I write of it in the past tense because, after twenty years of flowering, it died just before we left that garden. From it I learnt that white flowers, not bright flowers, give the greatest sense of space and liberation in a city when summer comes. Clear bright flowers are for the spring.

I planted mock orange too – scented and single varieties, not scentless and double like the one we inherited. These were *Philadelphus* 'Belle Etoile', gracefully arching, 3m (10ft) tall, with rows of wide open white flowers stained with a splash of wine behind the stamens, and *Philadelphus microphyllus*, shorter, less beautiful but more disciplined: 'Ideal for confined spaces', the catalogue description said. Not only were they easy, scented, and beautiful, but they gladly grew in deepest shade. With the growth of my mock oranges I at last became, like my neighbours, a secateurs gardener. As soon as flowering was over in July, before they had much chance to throw out their strong new growths, along I came purposefully with my secateurs and cut out all the flowering stems (some of them sticky now with blackfly) to make room for next year's replenishment of branches. How can it be that some people find the scent of philadelphus too strong and sweet? The stronger and sweeter the better, I say, if you live in a town.

Pale, scented flowers, then, on easy shrubs, were the ideal thing, and if, like philadelphus, they will grow in shade, so much the better. The aim was to have at least one flowering shrub for every season of the year. Some scents are there when you bend over the flowers until your nose touches the petals; other scents (like the scent of mock orange) hang on the air. This is what the best winter-flowerers do, offering a bonus in dull months; perhaps insects need extra inducement to attract them to winter flowers. Mahonia is an extraordinary shrub; I hated its large, rusty rosettes of dark green stiffly serrated leaves when first I saw them. Nor did I much admire its bunched racemes of yellow flowers. The small, ground-covering mahonias did not even seem to smell. But oh, *Mahonia japonica*! Here is lily-of-the-valley magnified, hanging on the air in January. We planted one in deep shade beside the twiggy philadelphus which had nothing to give in the winter months, and just beside the path so that one breathed the perfume on one's chilly way down to the rubbish bins. It brought a flurry of blue tits to the garden to swing among the yellow flowers and dull blue berries.

Daphne odora I loved from the start, remembering it in 'shoulder sprays' adorning the tailored lapels of Melbourne girls during the war years. The evergreen with cream-margined leaves, *Daphne odora* 'Aureomarginata', will survive for years in London in a warm corner, flowering from February onwards. I put one in a large earthenware pot and it is still growing there, spreading 1m (3ft) wide and 60cm (2ft) tall; its white and deep pink flowers look almost as if they were made of icing-sugar to go on cakes. And it takes the prize for scenting the air all around it: if you are trying to sell your house in winter, a sprig of daphne in a glass will scent a whole room and veil shabbiness with desirability. Its hardier English cousin, *Daphne mezereum*, does not yield up its scent so readily, nor has it so sweet a scent to yield. But its mauve-pink flowers along bare branches in winter have charm, and I welcomed it, and its seedlings, to a shady border.

After the winter-flowerers came ordinary things: the old white rhododendrons, the inherited white lilac, and forsythia.

PLATE 3 *The long and narrow space is broken here by a dark, hand-thrown pot which arrests your progress down the path under an arching branch of roses.*

Another lilac was not so much inherited as stolen – it was
a highly desirable low-growing variety, the small-leafed lilac,
Syringa microphylla 'Superba', whose scent makes you swoon
in May and again, with luck, in August. My knowledgeable old
neighbour had planted it; my unknowledgeable new neighbour,
who had bought the house and was engaged on a fatal 'clean
sweep', had dug it up. I spotted it on top of his rubbish heap and
stealthily, one evening, I lifted it over the wall and reinstated it in
our shady border. It had been out of the ground for some days
and I was prepared to watch it die, but it lived and prospered,
1.2m (4ft) high and 1m (3ft) wide, with miniature pink and
white lilac flowers among its pointed leaves, longer-lasting and
easier to see than the great panicles swaying half out of sight
on the branch tops of ordinary lilac. It was a much greater
asset than another May-flowering shrub I had chosen with
fastidious care: the apple-blossom tinted *Chaenomeles speciosa*
'Moerloesii', chosen because of my new-found preference for
pale flowers, but in the end less floriferous than the familiar
scarlet japonica.

At midsummer came the flowering of a foolproof shrub which
was generosity itself in blossoming. It was a deutzia, compact
and graceful, less than 1m (3ft) tall. Most of the year it looked
inconspicuous, merely a good-natured space-filler with twiggy
arching branches and narrow leaves. Then in June it mounted a
transformation scene: its arching twigs were alight with myriad
small, starry pink and white flowers. Deutzia is not fussy about
soil and will grow in half-shade although mine rejoiced in full
sun. The books and catalogues speak well of it. I saw it described
as 'very floriferous and reliable' (Notcutts), and a 'thoroughly
tough character' (Christopher Lloyd). It is related to the philadelphus and, like it, needs to be pruned back after flowering to

PLATE 4   *A seat in the sun faces south across the
same narrow garden, wreathed in* Carpenteria
californica *and roses.*

a point where a new shoot is breaking. I gladly did this for it, but so much did I take its generosity for granted that I am now uncertain whether it was *Deutzia discolor x* elegantissima that I grew, or another.

The pruning of shrubs is simple, or at least its timing is. If the shrub flowers on old wood in the first half of the year (like mock orange, japonica and deutzia) you cut back the flowering stems immediately the petals fall. If it flowers on new wood after midsummer, you prune it early in the spring. Hydrangeas belong to the second group. Its flowers come on the new green sappy growths, so you cut out some of last year's oldest growths altogether, down to the ground, and reduce a few others by a half. But most you behead only at the tip. In this way, so the books teach, you keep the plant replenished with new wood.

I became intolerant of the two cold pink hortensia hydrangeas I inherited. I decided I must have white ones (failing the incredible blue that only happens when the soil is fed with iron). I planted the splendid white hortensia 'Madame E. Mouillière', which was happy to flower in the shadow of the wall, and the smaller lacecap, *H. macrophylla* 'Lanarth White', less showy but more choice, with little fertile flowerets in the centre and large, pure white, sterile flowers round the edge of each corymb. They had to carry the garden in August when everything else was done – and round and through them graceful white Japanese anemones spread and towered, saving the garden from extinction at that deeply dusty, tired end-of-summer time.

The best season in the garden was of course the rose season, and the most cherished shrubs were the old roses. It was during my first decade of gardening that the fashion for old roses surfaced. It was just an enamoured whisper at first, but from discriminating quarters: it came from Sissinghurst into the *Observer*'s gardening columns, echoed in flower arrangements by Violet Stephenson and Constance Spry, both of whom wrote eloquently about their own gardens, wreathed in old roses, and about gardens they had known when they were young, where highly perfumed cabbage roses bloomed. Photographs of their arrangements showed marvellous mixtures inspired by the still-life flower paintings of the seventeenth-century Dutch school, where rounded, many-petalled shapes – paeonies, roses – provide the heart of the composition, with striped tulips and pinks, speckled foxgloves and dusky bearded irises breaking away round the edges, and adorned with butterflies and bees. I could not resist the allure of these roses glimpsed in oil paint, in black and white photographs, and in words. I had to have at least one. It would be more beautiful than I could imagine until I saw it. Nurserymen had begun to list them at the backs of their rose catalogues, behind the pages of hybrid teas and floribundas. 'Shrub roses', they were inclined to call them. Exhibitors at the RHS shows continued to concentrate on rounded vases of hybrid teas and floribundas, as before.

The two I chose were 'Fantin Latour', the Centifolia named after the great flower painter, and 'Mme Pierre Oger', the Bourbon whose bewitching shape I had identified in a photograph of mixed roses arranged by Constance Spry. 'Fantin Latour' proved to be a robust shrub, 1.8m (6ft) tall and 1.5m (5ft) wide with strong, healthy green leaves and clusters of pale pink flowers. The petals were tight-packed – there might well be a hundred to a flower to justify the label 'centifolia' – and they opened to a flat rosette 8cm (3in) across. Nothing could be more old-fashioned, less like the shape of modern roses, and perhaps I stifled a moment of disappointment as I realised that it lacked the deep cupped and furled shape of an HT rose. The scent was reassuringly sweet, however.

'Mme Pierre Oger' seemed frail in comparison, quite tall but slender and sometimes needing to be staked or tied together when her arching canes threatened to touch the ground. Her leaves were unremarkable, exhibiting the occasional touch of mildew or black spot. But the flowers were exquisite: sweetly fragrant, deeply cupped, with petals – each one like a translucent pink shell – arranged in perfect concentric circles. They reflexed inwards so that each flower was a little globe, slightly smaller than the wide open 'Fantin Latour' and better for picking, since their perfection of shape deserved a close-up view. Best of all, they were recurrent-flowering.

These two roses stood side by side among the bearded irises and behind the edging of pinks on the sunny side of the long garden. And then I realised that they were not alone, and that I had seen an 'old rose' before without knowing it. Further up this border and battling with the shade of the house was the rose on the long ungainly stem which we had dismissed as a 'giraffe'. We cut its leaning neck by half; it sent up new stems; it turned into 'William Lobb', the 'old velvet moss' with purple flowers and bright green mossy prickles. In time I learnt to like it. So three old roses, together with the irises and pinks, bloomed together. It was the best moment in the garden.

For this was also the moment of the hybrid musks. They are not properly classed as old roses, having been hybridised this century, but are the most serviceable of roses, big enough to make a real statement, and they were of unique importance in our garden. With them I made a barrier (I only needed two plants with which to do it) between the lawn and the square of paving at the bottom of the garden, in an attempt to break up the monotony of our ground plan. Musk roses are a beginner's dream: healthy, pretty, obligingly easy to prune, repeat-flowering and divinely perfumed. They belong to that favoured category of plants whose scent hangs upon the air. I chose the variety 'Cornelia', believing it to be less vigorous than the famous trio: 'Penelope', 'Buff Beauty' and 'Felicia'. In fact it spread out 1.5m (5ft) to left and right, and grew about 1.5m (5ft) tall. Its heavy trusses of rosette-shaped flowers were apricot in bud, pink fading to cream in blossom, and its young foliage had a beautiful copper tinge. When the first flush of rapturous June flowering was over, out came the secateurs. 'Cut back to encourage new growth and a second

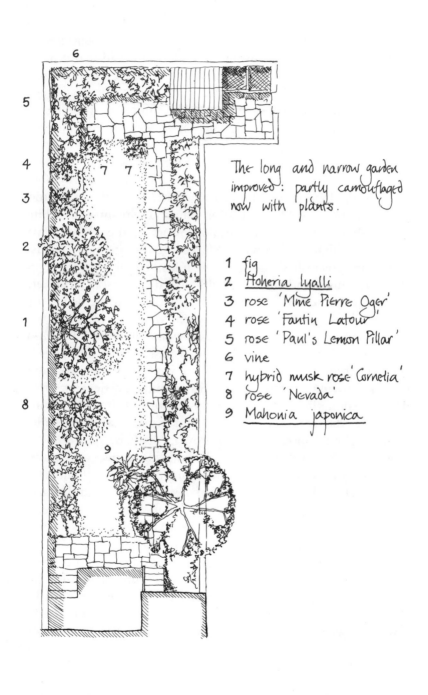

The long and narrow garden
improved: partly camouflaged
now with plants.

1 fig
2 _Hoheria lyalli_
3 rose 'Mme Pierre Oger'
4 rose 'Fantin Latour'
5 rose 'Paul's Lemon Pillar'
6 vine
7 hybrid musk rose 'Cornelia'
8 rose 'Nevada'
9 _Mahonia japonica_

blooming', I said to myself, snipping every single spent cluster back to just above a promising leaf axil (I had read that it must be a leaf composed of five leaflets, not three). I can't pretend that the second blooming was ever quite a match for the first.

The pruning of hybrid musks is one thing, the pruning of climbing roses quite another, and yet I had to have climbing roses. The walls had to be clothed. Space is short even in a garden 27m (90ft) long, and none of it must be wasted. There was room for a rose in the corner along a stretch of reasonably sunny wall. It must not be too vigorous; it must not be too bright. It must be 'Paul's Lemon Pillar', a dream of a white rose with voluptuous, substantial flowers in the HT shape I longed for, high-centred with reflexed edges to its many petals, ivory with greenish shadows in the folds. The flowers came in clusters, scented and abundant, although their season was brief.

Up into the dead laburnum tree on the shady side of the garden I sent another climbing rose: 'Mme Alfred Carrière', a so-called continuous bloomer, its white flowers loose and unshowy compared with those of 'Paul's Lemon Pillar' – a countrified, old-fashioned rose. There is a famous photograph of it smothering a whole wall at Sissinghurst Castle; our Mme Alfred, leaning half-reluctantly into the fork of the dead laburnum tree, did not look like that, but remains a wonderfully strong, obliging rose, willing to grow in shade or sun.

We had four other successful climbers against our walls. The first was that boon of town gardeners, the self-clinging, shade-tolerant beauty, *Hydrangea petiolaris*. It sounded too good to be true when I first read of it, but it *was* true. I planted it in deep shade against the old dark bricks, and it arranged its fresh green leaves in horizontal lines along them, crawling rapidly over the decaying lines of mortar as if it knew how to espalier itself, then sending vertical shoots upwards until there was a neat chequering of branching stems, half-hidden by the bright hydrangea leaves and pretty white and green lacecap flowers. It would have spread indefinitely along that dreary wall, but it had to be checked to make room for a second beautiful, easy, shade-loving climber.

This was *Vitis henryana*, now called *Parthenocissus henryana*, since its self-clinging habit makes it a Virginia creeper rather than a vine. I planted it behind the lily-of-the-valley near the back door, and it eventually covered that wall and set off, tidily and gracefully, up the house wall as well, until long garlands of it began to swing down, not making a nuisance of themselves, just decorating a dark corner. Its palmate leaves are strangely decorative, stylishly veined in white and pink on a background of dusky green, shading to garnet in October.

For brilliant autumn colour (a difficult thing to achieve in a London garden) we planted a true member of the vine family: *Vitis coignetiae*. Its huge heart-shaped leaves, thick as parchment, turn from pleasant green to cherry and coral and flame before they fall. We gave it the sunny retaining wall in the front garden and attempted to teach it where it should go with wall nails and wire. Each year its exuberance made fun of our plans, and its long tendrils waved freely in the air. It was a joyous but untidy sight. Properly trained, it is a winner.

Finally, we planted a real grape vine. It filled the space where the winter sweet failed to spread on the sunny wall across the bottom of our garden. I chose the variety called 'Hamburgh' because I did not know that 'Brant' would fruit better. Grape vines are like figs, bringing a sense of warmth and good living to English town gardens, even without grapes. But in warm summers, small bunches of grapes came. Like all vines, this one grew quickly; in February the side shoots were pruned back to two or three eyes and in April the lovely fresh green leaves burst forth and gave the suggestion of plenty to the garden's end. Its energy was limitless, despite the fact that it had only a handful of bonemeal and a shovel full of our indifferent compost to nourish it each spring.

It may sound as if the walls of our garden were now well clothed. They were not. The idea was to 'plant the walls out', to make a wilderness so that one could not quite tell where the garden ended. In practice one could tell exactly where it ended on every flank, despite the climbers, despite the fig tree, despite the hybrid musk roses: the basic brick rectangle remained.

And what of ground level? What of edging plants to break the hard lines of path and lawn? My greatest success was sweet woodruff (*Asperula odorata*). I acquired one little plant which spread all along the edge of the shady border in the neatest possible way, always ready to fill gaps, always easy to pull out where it was not wanted, with white starry flowers and green starry leaves.

My next success was *Heuchera cylindrica* 'Greenfinch'. It was easy to divide as an edging to sunny paving: indeed, it needed to be divided if it was to retain its satisfactory shape (fat clumps of beautiful, slightly marbled round leaves). Its wiry stems rose tall in summer from these basal rosettes of leaves and the pale green flowers looked good with 'Paul's Lemon Pillar' roses in a vase.

Then there was rue, *Ruta graveolens* 'Jackman's Blue'. Its smell is bitter, and its literary associations are bitter too. 'There's rue for you, and here's some for me . . .' said mad Ophelia to the unhappy Queen. But the colour and shape of its glaucous blue leaves tempts one to override tragic associations and give it an important place beside the paving.

And then there was a hosta. The great thing about hostas is the contrast they provide when placed at a border's edge; those large, overlapping leaves curve strongly forwards and make other edging plants like sweet woodruff look simply fuzzy. Only one hosta is needed to make this point; it is a punctuation point, a pause for the eye before looking on along a path. Mine was the well-tried favourite *Hosta sieboldiana*, its blue-green leaves beautifully ribbed in parallel lines, almost as if fluted by a skilful dressmaker. The pale spires of bell-shaped flowers are fine but transitory, becoming ragged at the bottom before the topmost bells have opened; it is the leaves one remembers.

Between the edging plants and the shrubs and climbers the border flowers came and went. In winter *Helleborus corsicus* never failed in a shady corner; indeed, it seeded itself generously, even growing out of old mortar in the walls, always with its showy heads of budgerigar-green flowers lasting for weeks and weeks (though dying immediately if cut for the house). In spring, the wands of Solomon's seal (*Polygonatum multiflorum*) arched over the lily-of-the-valley in a large-scale mimicry of its fresh green and white colour scheme. Like the lilies-of-the-valley, it spread a little further each year. This was a happy combination.

In summer came a major *coup*: tree paeonies (*Paeonia suffruticosa*). Clumps of herbaceous paeonies, the pink 'Sarah Bernhardt', the pearly 'Lady Alexander Duff', flowered for a year or two in the borders, then petered out, but the tree paeonies grew and their woody stems multiplied. Perhaps the secret was good drainage, for they were planted in a shallow bed over the old coal cellar by the front steps. Or perhaps they are not difficult to grow, just expensive. At any rate they were worth their cost; their combination of size and delicacy takes the breath away. Their flowers are 13cm (5in) across, yet look almost too fragile to touch. One of them was pink, 'Lord Selborne', the other, 'Mrs William Kelway', was white. As they grew, I tied their stems to the black iron railings which stood behind them as ready-made stakes. Their deeply cut leaves were soft grey-green, their petals seemed made of pure silk and their stamens of gold-dust. They smelt exotically of musk. Non-gardening visitors who stood on our front steps in May marvelled at them, and gardening visitors rejoiced.

So there it was. Many lovely plants lived brief lives in this long garden. A few settled down confidently and made it their own. Some of these are no doubt still living there today. But after five years of planting, a change came over the garden. There was a pram on the lawn.

This pram signalled further changes: a sandpit on the

sunny paving, a swing beside the philadelphus, a scarlet and blue climbing frame standing obtrusively beside the fig tree. A black mongrel dog raced up and down the straight and boring lawn, wearing a path to the rubbish bins. A striped cat picked her way through the plants and scaled the old walls. A goldfish was buried at the foot of the vine. A tortoise peeped from under the hosta leaves. It was lucky now that the garden was so uncomplicated; it suited the children and their pets at play.

When you have children, you get to know your neighbours. My planting days, my days of discovery and experiment, were curtailed for the moment; the garden had to survive on two or three widely spaced onslaughts a year. But I began to gain admission to other people's gardens.

V

The Long and Narrow

Parts answ'ring parts shall slide into a whole
Alexander Pope, Epistle IV: Of the Use of Riches

Grove Terrace was built between 1790 and 1820. As you went up the hill, the houses became earlier, Regency gave way to Georgian, there were little wrought-iron balconies at the first-floor windows and exquisitely varied fanlights between classical pillars and beneath pediments which were sometimes pointed and sometimes flat. The terrace faced south-west, and on winter afternoons the plane trees in the municipal gardens opposite cast a tracery of shadows over the brick façades. The back gardens were mostly very long, about 36m (120ft), running almost out of sight under old pear trees, yews, hollies and hawthorns. Birds flew down from Hampstead Heath to find rich pickings; brilliant, raucous jays landed briefly on the lawns in the day time; and often owls hooted, breaking through our dreams at night. Beyond the gardens was a back access lane lined with garage doors and weeds, the remains of compost heaps and bonfires, bits of michaelmas daisy and comfrey, blackberries and seedling sycamores. We used to call it 'the country lane'.

The first garden I got to know there belonged to my elderly aunt, Bunny. She came to live in the terrace in 1957, the year our first baby was born. Her house was divided into two flats, with curious old bathrooms and heavy embossed wallpaper.

'It's a good buy,' we said. 'Look at the ceiling mouldings, the Gothic stained-glass window, the mirror panels on the doors. Freehold.' Doubtfully, she looked. She had been thinking of a modern leasehold maisonette in Paddington. But the long garden trapped her in its net of possibilities. Her subsequent arrival meant for me an extension of my gardening knowledge and a whole extra length of terraced garden with which to be involved.

She belonged to mother's classification of 'great gardeners'. She came bringing with her from Warwickshire a few rare and beloved plants: a twining climber called *Akebia quinata*; an edging plant called *Poterium tenuifolium*, a burnet with pretty soft green foliage which she called 'bottlebrush'; a beloved old rose, the alba 'Céleste', which she claimed was the most exquisite pink rose she knew. She also brought an old teak garden seat, and set about the heady task of making an alien territory her own.

People's gardens reflect their temperaments. Where Eileen was positive, impulsive and easily distracted, my aunt Bunny was tentative and meditative, impressionable and slow. This meant that she read the garden writers in her chosen papers with humble open-mindedness, often cutting out their columns and sometimes passing them on to me. She also listened to *Gardeners' Question Time* on the radio and repeated the occasional tip. 'You can move a plant at the wrong time,' she told me, 'in the middle of the summer, if you fill the new planting hole with a kettle full of boiling water first and let it drain away before you put the plant in. They say it won't even droop. I've tried it and it works!'

In those days, Vita Sackville-West ruled the roost from the pages of the *Observer*. We spoke of her as a friend. 'Vita', Bunny would say, 'recommends the climbing rose "Cupid". A lovely *single* rose.' Bunny made pilgrimages to Sissinghurst, driving slowly from North London to Kent in her Morris Minor. She returned with notes of the plants she admired. One such plant was *Hydrangea villosa*: she saw it against a wall, loved it, noted it, ordered it from a nurseryman and in due course planted it. It began to spread out wide against one of her own garden walls, a huge fan with long, elegant pointed leaves of sober, felted sage green; in August it was suddenly spectacular with its airy lacecap flowers like lavender stars surrounding pincushions of intense blue. Bunny was mute with pride while I was loud with praise; I half-felt that she was personally responsible for the astonishing beauty of this shrub, and recognised that she was indeed a 'great gardener'.

It was plants she loved; her intelligence prompted her to search for them, read about them and view them, and her taste led her to choose well. Reserved and unsure of herself with people, she had no inhibitions about plants, allowing herself to use emotionally charged words in describing them: 'adorable . . . exquisite . . . ravishing . . .'

When she moved in, her garden was rather shaggy, without any notable plants in it. It turned out to have a path down the right-hand side, invisible under grass. We scraped and clawed the grass back with spade and trowel and fingers; it rolled away to reveal an underside of closely matted roots like the wrong side of a doormat, and underneath was brick paving with an edging of slate-grey Victorian tiles with scalloped tops. The only trees were a variegated holly and a dowdy English yew growing by one wall. She accepted these old evergreens with affectionate gratitude, and decided that the yew would serve admirably to screen the little garden shed she had planned. This shed was her first essential improvement: small, neat and smelling of creosote, it was erected in the shadow of the yew and housed her cherished tools: her lady's border fork with short, widely spaced prongs, its handle polished from holding; her spade, rakes, stainless-steel trowel, her stiff broom, her 'kneeler' with tubular-steel supports designed to help the elderly hoist themselves to their feet, her aluminium tongs for picking up garden rubbish, her balls of tarred string, her new electric mower. Everything had its proper place; there were hooks to hang things on so that they did not have to clutter up the floor. You could tell, from her shed, that she meant business.

But she had no confidence in designing the layout of the garden. Fortunately, beneath the unkempt mess, there was a lovely sequence. 'My garden has five chapters!' she said with awe when she moved in. The first chapter, near the house, was paved. It had a small round bed in it, which I thought fussy and old-fashioned, but she did not presume to change it. She put a little pyramid of clipped box in it (which later died round the bottom because of the attentions of tom cats). Then came a short section of grass with a curved path through it and a second small round flower bed which she did, reluctantly, eliminate, filling it in with grassy turves cut from the edges. Chapter III was a small sunken garden, with two steps down and paved. It was edged with tall flag irises, and felt as if it ought to be a pond. Up two steps again, and on went the garden into a sunlit chapter beyond the shadow cast by the terrace houses; here was a long strip of lawn and a sunny border beside it where all the best herbaceous plants were to grow: delphiniums, day lilies, sidalcea, phlox and musk roses.

In the narrow shady border opposite she grew auriculas, looking as though they were cut out of Victorian velvet, ferns, dead nettle, London pride and foxgloves. When my children were toddlers she made them purple finger-tips out of fallen foxglove flowers. 'That's why they're called "fox*gloves*",' she told them, as they stretched out their Strewel-Peter hands.

Lying beneath spotted laurels and among old yew needles in this shady border was a thrilling discovery: a slab of Coade stone, with a recumbent female figure on it in bas-relief, its legs swathed in becoming neo-classical draperies, a palette and brushes in one hand. The Muse of Painting? She knew this treasure must be mounted somewhere in the garden and was easily persuaded to have a low dividing wall built across the far end of the sunny stretch of lawn; it curved up to hold the rectangular bas-relief. Below this wall she placed the old teak seat; you could sit there in the sun and look back down the garden's length. Over the wall she trained the vigorously lovely climbing rose 'Lawrence Johnston', which in June spilled its loose sunshine-yellow flowers and pointed buds over the Muse of Painting.

And behind the wall came the final chapter: 'the wilderness', she called it. Here she planted the wild-looking rose 'Frühlingsmorgen' among self-seeding balsam and long grasses. The sight of this rose, much taller than me, smothered in its wide single flowers, pink with wine-red stamens against cream centres, filled me with wonder and admiration in May as *Hydrangea villosa* did in August.

Bunny's garden gradually filled up with roses. She found old-fashioned roses which would grow on the shady side of the path as well as in the sun. But she was not an old-rose snob; she also planted a floribunda, 'Sweet Repose', opening warm cream edged with pink. Like me, she planted the hybrid musk 'Cornelia'; she grew the mighty climber 'Mermaid' up her north-facing wall. They all flowered prodigiously, an affirmation that life is worth living, a bulwark against doubt and loneliness.

She was sixty-nine when she started to enrich and replant her terrace garden, and eighty-three when she died. In the intervening years, when I paid my hasty visits, she was sometimes sitting in her armchair upstairs under the moulded plaster ceiling and beside the electric fire, but more often she was in her garden, wearing her curious ankle-high gumboots and her velveteen gardening beret, bending, stretching, cutting, digging, forking, tying up with string, or shuffling up and down her patches of grass behind her lightweight electric mower, her mind on her garden and her plans for the future.

When we persuaded Bunny to build a low wall to house her Coade stone slab, we were using our neighbour's garden as a model. For five years I had been looking down on that garden where the blue cranesbill and the purple *Campanula glomerata* grew. Peeping from an upstairs window, I had thought how clever was its answer to the question of the long and narrow garden. Two-thirds of the way down it was divided by a low brick wall in which was set a wrought-iron gate. The gate was tall, and so the low wall curved upwards on either side of it to form a pair of brick gateposts. Roses climbed over the walls to left and right, and you could not see what lay on the other side until you passed through the gate. You walked down the garden and through the gate along a wide flagstone path; to your left was a wide mixed border, to your right a lawn reaching right up to the boundary wall. Through the gate you discovered a paved rose garden. It was a simple design, but much less obvious than ours; its balance of asymmetry with symmetry was exactly right. How daring seemed the decision to omit a border altogether on the shady side, and to make the border on the sunny side twice as wide! I envied the border's width, and saw how stultifyingly narrow our borders were. I envied the big flagstones, and felt discontented with our crazy paving. I envied that slightly absurd yet picturesque wall and gate, and the sense of a secret garden beyond.

The guiding principle of designing a long, narrow garden seemed now quite clear to me. You simply divided it crossways. You could divide it halfway along, or a third of the way along, or two-thirds of the way along, or you could divide it twice or even three times if it was very long. The divisions could be built with bricks, or made by living things. But you should not be able to see the whole of a long garden at once, and it should not be the same all the way down. It should come, as Bunny would say, in chapters.

Two families living further along the terrace, in whose gardens our children played, had found memorably simple solutions to the problem, in each case with a single division of the garden's length. In the first (one of the shortest in the whole row) a group of weeping silver birches, three or four of them, were planted two-thirds of the way down the lawn. They were slender, graceful space-dividers, veiling without obliterating the garden view.

In the second, which was much longer, there were borders down each side, but a third of the way down the garden the borders moved towards each other briefly, forming brief straits through which the visitor could sail. Two groups of shrubs did the trick: it seemed that they had been planted opposite each other and had simply decided that they must have more room, and begun to lean outwards from their borders so that you could barely see beyond them. They were unremarkable things: a berberis, a fern, a deutzia, an azalea, a variegated weigela, most of them grown from cuttings. This was Joanna's garden. As a child during the war, she had helped her mother grow vegetables; they had dug together for victory. She believed in plants, trusted them, stuck cuttings blithely into the earth, watered them and watched over them and expected them to grow. She did not, like me, see gardening as shopping; she saw it as a natural process and as friendly barter, where you swopped bits of this and that with gardening friends. Her borders were tight-packed with large and flourishing shrubs grown from cuttings, herbaceous clumps grown from small divisions, favourite roses from birthday presents, and a very few purchases. The result was like a cottage garden, unpremeditated, where a devoted gardener laboured, regarding all her plants with affectionate tolerance and mothering them with successful homemade compost twice a year. The garden picture had effortless charm: a green, wavering corridor of grass beckoned you forwards between ranks of flowers, through the narrow isthmus where the shrubs spilled forward, until finally you reached an old-fashioned oval rose bed beneath a pear tree which was there when Joanna came and which she saw no reason to change.

When she moved in, a few years later than Bunny, she too had found an overgrown garden with a path down one side.

The path was made of stone, but she disliked it; she grudged the
space it occupied, and the fact that, tucked in beside a narrow
border as it was, nobody ever walked on it. Her children ran
straight down the middle of the lawn instead. She levered up
the flagstones, big and small, and carted some of them through
the house and paved the front garden with them. Some of the
smaller ones she reused as widely spaced stepping stones down
the middle of the garden where people usually walked, and with
the rest she made a terrace just outside the back door where the
morning sun shone warmly. Then, from side to side, from border
to border, she sowed grass. It was the line of stepping stones set
in grass that became the beckoning corridor which led the eye
onwards, down the garden, accentuating rather than concealing
its length. The eye always follows the line of a lawn.

This unselfconscious garden with its pretty mixture of plants
imperilled my newly formulated principle of garden design. It
seemed to say: Don't worry. Just make room for lovely plants
and the plants will do the rest. They will do the dividing up of
the garden for you.

But then I got to know another terraced garden, where the
lesson of division seemed to have been well learnt. An enthusiastic handyman had divided up the garden architecturally,
by building a low concrete circle halfway down his garden.
It enclosed a circle of paving, in the middle of which stood an
urn. There were two breaks in the circle so that a path could
cut right through it to the other side. But if you were following
the path down the garden you had a problem: you came slap up
against the urn. It made a maddeningly complex obstacle race
when my eldest daughter and her 'best friend' began to play
there. As the years went by, however, the concrete weathered
and the whole thing took on a sort of grandeur; it was a case
of every man his own Versailles.

The house and garden had been bought by the parents of my
daughter's friend. The vexing question was: should this circular
construction stay or go? Was it rather attractive or was it rather

awful? The father quite liked it, the mother didn't. They asked their friendly neighbour, a distinguished landscape architect, for his advice. Unhesitatingly he advised that it should go.

What was the matter with it, I wondered (for I had privately agreed with the father in this debate)? After all, it broke up the length of the garden, providing an interesting and decidedly unusual focal point halfway down. Yes, but it was so arbitrary, that was its trouble. It did not relate to anything – not to the house, nor to the brick boundary walls, nor to the trees that came over from neighbours' gardens. Geoffrey Jellicoe (the friendly landscape architect) suggested a series of three simple spaces to replace the condemned concrete circle. Near the house were to be two generous borders separated by a flagstone path. This should give way to lawn, a peaceful expanse of grass spreading from wall to wall and punctuated by three trees: a tree of heaven (*Ailanthus altissima*), an *Amelanchier canadensis* and, against the south-facing wall, an espaliered pear. Beyond the lawn and concealing a garden shed was to be what it amused him to term a 'bosquet': a small thicket of trees and shrubs.

When this garden was duly planted it proved not strident, not seeking to attract attention, but just satisfying and right, a peaceful place to be. Clearly, the idea that all you have to do with a long and narrow garden is to divide it up in any way you like was an over-simplification: a long garden should be a sequence of spaces which relate to each other, and finally coalesce to form a single composition.

There was another eminent architect and town planner living in Grove Terrace in the 1950s. Frederick Gibberd made a garden there before he moved to Harlow and constructed a six-acre garden on the edge of the New Town he had created. He later described garden-making as 'a selfish, intense and absorbing pleasure'. At Grove Terrace he produced a triumphant solution to a series of problems: not only the problem of the long, narrow garden, but the problem of reconciling a play space for children with an outdoor room for adults, and the enduring problem of making a garden that would rise above the cycles of change and decay and the dullness of a London winter, and look good all year round.

Gibberd would not have applied the word 'chapters' to the divisions of a garden; he might have preferred the word 'rooms', for he thought not in literary but in architectural terms. *Space* emerged as the key concept in skilled garden designing. The difference between this and my mechanical, rule-of-thumb approach was as crucial as the difference between a positive and a negative photograph. A long garden should indeed be compartmented, but the means used to divide it were of only incidental importance; just as the area of a room is more important than its walls, so the important thing here was the series of spaces itself. And just as, in a well-designed house, there is pleasure in passing from one room to the next and pain if two adjoining rooms clash with each other, so in a garden, one space should give way to the next as an apparently inevitable evolution. There is a further complication: whatever you use as a wall to signal the end of one garden room will need to become, on its other side, a suitable background for the next compartment.

Gibberd's garden had four rooms, fluid rooms, like the divisions in an open-plan house. The dividers were partial – they never extended right across the garden, and two of them were low. At one point he used a very low privet hedge neatly to mark the end of a stretch of lawn, the clipped vertical wall of green in perfect accord with the small stretch of mown grass leading up to it. On the far side of the clipped privet was a simple bench of the same length as the hedge and just a little lower than it – a bench of exactly the right height for small children to sit on, and facing a gravelled area where a sandpit and a stone trough invited children to play. The sandpit itself was hidden from the house by a low stone wall on which was mounted a wooden trellis for climbing plants.

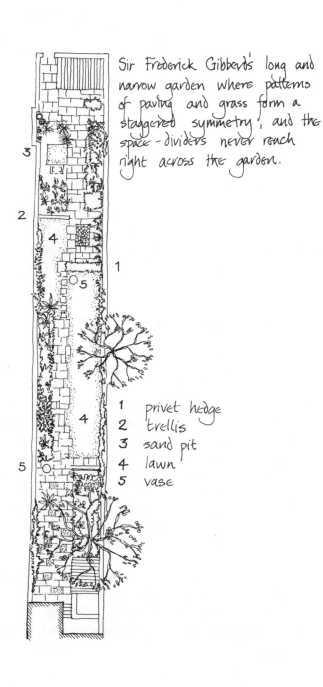

Sir Frederick Gibberd's long and
narrow garden where patterns
of paving and grass form a
staggered symmetry, and the
space-dividers never reach
right across the garden.

1   privet hedge
2   trellis
3   sand pit
4   lawn
5   vase

Stone paving, mown grass, clipped privet, pebbles, gravel, a bamboo screen, wooden trellises and two large simple vases were the elements out of which Gibberd made his garden, and the dominant one of these was the paving. It ran from end to end of the garden – a boon for tricycle riders. There were delightful hazards, very slight changes of level over which the skilled rider might bump, and changes in direction too; first you had to ride along the left-hand side of the garden, and then along the right.

The first compartment of this garden was a wide paved terrace of Purbeck stone near the house, with one or two rectangles of pebbles set into it; up a low step, and the paving became simply a broad path of York slabs with an uneven edge dictated by the random size of the slabs, with a narrow border on its left and a length of lawn on its right. Before this lawn came to an end (at the privet hedge) a second lawn had started on the left, and the path shrank to a single paving stone in width; for a few yards it became a narrow path between two, staggered lawns. When the right-hand lawn stopped the left-hand lawn continued for a few more paces until it, too, met a barrier: the creeper-covered trellis screening the sandpit. But the path had already seemed obliged to swing towards the right on the far side of the privet, as if paving, like air or water, must expand to fill a threatening vacuum. And so the paving stones continued for a few yards on the right, then up another shallow step, and at the very bottom of the garden they spread out once more into a terrace, filling the whole width of the garden from wall to wall, a place where the parents and their friends could sit in the afternoon sun, removed from the children yet keeping an eye on them. Here the south-facing wall was painted white, the trapped sun was reflected, and a beautiful seat with a tiled top was sunk into the wall.

This garden was an abstract composition, a pattern of rectangles in different sizes and relations to each other, over-lapping, asymmetric, brilliantly balanced, all held within the original long rectangle of the site. Nothing seemed arbitrary:

the shifting of the path from left to right seemed as inevitable as the placing of the steps; though everything was geometric, there was no monotonous repetition; the right-hand lawn was longer than the one on the left. A journey down the garden was a discovery: you could not tell what lay beyond the staggered screens. Paradoxically, the weaving layout of the path made the walk down the garden longer, while concealing the garden's length.

Plants here were part of the pattern, each carefully placed. The borders where they grew were narrow, and leaves were large, or finely cut, or evergreen: a fig trained against a whitewashed wall near the house, hostas, ferns, hollyhocks, a Japanese maple. Big trees in neighbours' gardens gave leafiness; an ancient hawthorn near the back door gave shade. There were no herbaceous plants, and the only roses climbed high on a south-facing trellis out of harm's way.

This brilliant piece of garden design has remained in my memory for nearly three decades. I first met it in a book – one of the library books I most often borrowed from my public library. Little did I suspect, when I pored over its photographs and plan, that the original existed a few yards from where I sat. It is an example of a garden where design is supreme, taking into account all obstacles and evolving as an answer to them. It would be valid in winter and summer, defeating time through mastery of space.

In contrast, the Jellicoes' garden a few doors down was the child of time. For Geoffrey Jellicoe, the potential of the site was not its walls but the trees beyond its walls. He wanted to recapture the country in this strip of town, and even to recapture the past, a feeling of return to nature, to the mysterious forest which, he believed, still exists in the human subconscious. He wanted to be able to lie on the grass in summer and feel, looking up through branches of trees, that he was in a forest glade. There were already three trees in the garden when the Jellicoes moved in in 1939: a towering ash, an energetic sycamore, and a fig. He welcomed them all three. The fig was allowed to grow larger and leafier each year until its branches crossed the garden and met the ash on the other side. When at last the ash tree died, the sycamore beyond it was large enough to take its place. The pattern of the garden shifted a little and settled down to its slightly adjusted system of weights and balances. He watched, with intense interest rather than dismay, the re-emerging patterns of light and shade, of open space and confinement, which these cycles of life and death brought with them. To him, garden-making had to take place with acceptance of change, not defiance of it.

His design was simple. The end of the garden nearest the house should be full of flowers, for Susan Jellicoe was an expert flower-gardener and she should have what women, he believed, had demanded since the Middle Ages: a compact garden filled with flowers from side to side. Beyond that was to be an axial lawn – a stretch of grass that would draw you onwards – which he called a 'philosopher's walk'. It would lead you round the fig towards your goal – a secret garden (the *giardino segreto*) where you could rest. To go behind a white garden seat made by Gordon Russell he designed a white trellis with squares a third as wide again as they were high, to exaggerate the garden's width. Then he had high wattle hurdles built round three sides of this space so that the secret feeling would be safe. The fourth side was the fig tree. And behind the seat and its screen of wattles were the tool shed and the compost heap. That was all – the rest was Susan Jellicoe's planting.

She planted out the walls with shrubs and climbers. There were roses, of course, and honeysuckle, clematis and jasmine, ivies and a Russian vine; there were *Paeonia lutea* and *Hydrangea paniculata*. The garden merged into the neighbours' gardens; if you stood on the lawn in summer, you seemed to be in one huge spreading garden space, full of trees – what Geoffrey Jellicoe has called a 'marvellous green city'. It was a studied

Sir Geoffrey Jellicoe's long and narrow garden: a philosopher's walk between steadily dwindling borders which make the garden seem wider instead of narrower as it recedes from view.

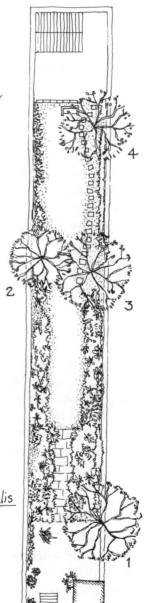

1 Prunus subhirtella autumnalis
2 fig
3 ash
4 sycamore

illusion: you were to imagine that this was not London, but Arcadia.

In winter, of course, came disillusionment: neighbouring houses reappeared, other people's garden sheds and garages could be seen. But a winter-flowering cherry, *Prunus subhirtella autumnalis*, planted nearer to the house than the forest trees, grew larger each year until, in its maturity, it threw its gracefully arching branches right across the garden, and for anyone looking from a window the view was framed in an exquisite tracery of fragile white blossom. If the beauty of this miraculous winter tree drew you into the garden, you found flourishing clumps of hellebores at its feet.

When you first came through the back door in summer, your view down the garden was half-obscured by bamboo – not this time a bamboo screen as in Frederick Gibberd's garden, but a living bamboo grove of the elegant and comparatively non-invasive *Arundinaria murieliae*. Big pots of arching hardy fuchsias (*F. magellanica* 'alba') with pale cream dangling trumpets stood round you, *Alchemilla mollis* seeded itself everywhere in concrete cracks, and you began your walk between herbaceous borders.

Flowers near the house, and a veiled glimpse of grass beyond, is a happier thing than its opposite, and the smaller the garden, the more important it is to have your first glimpse of it half-obscured by a close-up of flowers. Susan Jellicoe's mixed borders were 12m (40ft) long; they were separated by a stone path, and had the rightness of all twin borders, in which there is a classic satisfaction in walking down a path in early June between clumps of herbaceous flowers. There were sprawling oriental poppies and pointed lupins, valerian and ox-eye daisies, with the towering spires of *Macleaya cordata* at the back and the fat round leaves of *Anchusa myosotidiflora*, bergenia and cranesbill at the front. But Susan Jellicoe did not practise rigid grading of plants by height. She allowed tall plants at the front of the borders too, so that the photogenic shapeliness of their profiles could be seen. There were bearded irises, day lilies, and a 'wealth of globed paeonies . . .', in particular the paeony 'Baroness Schroeder', carrying its huge flowers aloft, high above its leaves, each one a handspan across, a shell-pink many-petalled globe.

At the start of your journey down the garden, finding yourself surrounded by archetypal country flowers, there was a sort of excitement: you hovered, looking first to one side then the other. But all the time the lawn's magnetic field was drawing you on, and when you reached it you had no choice but to pass down the philosopher's walk, suddenly feeling free of bonds, through sunshine towards deep shadow. Now the borders dwindled, from 3m (9ft) to a mere 1m (3ft) where the path ended and the lawn began, and by the time you penetrated the secret garden beyond the fig tree they had almost disappeared. This calculated perspective of ever-diminishing borders corrected the tendency of a long garden to get narrower towards the end.

When you reached the secret garden, you did not want to hover or to walk, but to sit in tranquillity, hidden from view. The grass spread in front of you right to the hurdles on either side, but along the edges self-seeding wild flowers – foxgloves and Tibetan balsam – were allowed to grow, and lily-of-the-valley and periwinkle to spread.

'This is all so natural,' I was inclined to feel, 'so simple, I could have thought of it myself.'

But I hadn't thought of it myself. It occupied a different gardening world from mine. Its naturalness lay not so much in being obvious as in being harmonious, its simplicity the result of an artist's unifying vision.

VI

Front Gardens and Basement Gardens

Belbroughton Road is bonny, and pinkly bursts the spray
Of prunus and forsythia across the public way.

John Betjeman, 'May-Day Song for North Oxford'

A privet hedge and a neat square of lawn beside a straight flagstone path: this was the Jellicoes' front garden. 'Very dull,' I used to think as I walked past up the hill to the library. I was teaching myself horticulture from other people's front gardens. Long before I saw those endlessly stimulating back gardens, I was on familiar terms with the fronts.

They were pocket-handkerchief gardens, with straight short paths up to their front doors and area railings below the ground-floor windows. Once there would have been black iron railings along the street as well, and later a succession of neat privet hedges, but the railings were melted down for munitions in World War II, and the privet was now beginning to give way to less tailored hedges of escallonia or berberis or to no hedges at all. Neat uniformity and a sense of street architecture, translated into horticulture, had gone. Individuality and tentative gardening experiments were everywhere.

The gardens that we walk past in our routine days join the stack of indelible images which pattern our inner lives. Even for non-gardeners, hurrying past with heads bowed, the spirit is saddened by neglected plots where the rubbish bins stand amongst dead leaves, and the mood momentarily lightened by bright window boxes and flowering trees. For gardeners, the experience is conscious. Instead of being sunk in private thoughts, we gardeners are on a quest, looking sideways at the gardens that we pass, hoping against hope that *today* they will be looking better, and always knowing that, a little further on round the next corner, is a really nice garden. It is a case of discontent and disappointment, punctuated by fixed points of pleasure.

At number five the owner dug up his front lawn and replaced it with a carpet of heather; in flower, it was as joyless as dry pink plastic sponge, but it proclaimed itself as trouble-free. Unhappy, I hurried past. This was the time when gardeners were being advised to scrap their front lawns; carting the mowing machine through the house was recognised as an avoidable burden. At number eight an elderly man dug up his grass too and laid crazy paving set in concrete with a neat round hole in the middle. In it he placed a single plant – a mop-headed pink hydrangea; in autumn its leaves looked rusty, and in winter its stems looked formless. It had not the character, the shape or grace, to carry off its important position in the middle of a bed in the middle of a garden with no other plants to help it. It needed to be with others of its kind, at the edge of a shady border.

But then, at number six, in a dark garden behind a spotted laurel hedge and a bit of dusty holly, a beautiful rose began to flower. It was a climber, trained along the area railings. 'I've found out what that beautiful rose is at number six!' said Bunny in excitement one summer. 'It's called "Meg"!' 'Meg' was large and nearly single, with red stamens against petals the colour of chamois leather touched with apricot. She redeemed the garden where she grew, and joined the shortlist of lovely plants that gave hope to my walks.

Up the slope at number twenty-five I identified *Cotoneaster horizontalis* for the first time. Here, the area railings had been abolished, the front garden had been excavated to allow light into the basement windows, and there was a small new bed beside the front path held in place by a brick retaining wall that went down about 2.5m (8ft) to basement level. This vertical drop was countered by the horizontal branching of the cotoneaster. It was never allowed an upward-pointing stem. Its function was to fan outwards, masking the brick edging of its bed with ever-increasing and extending tiers of twiggery. Like the hydrangea further down the hill, it was alone in its small bed; unlike the hydrangea, it was shapely all year round, not least in winter, when its red berries remained after the fall of its small dark leaves, garnet-red in autumn, and the delicate detail of its fish-bone structure, stiff yet lacy, was revealed. This was architectural planting. (It turned out to be Sir Frederick Gibberd's front garden.)

At number nine, a bustling new family moved in. There were small children, musical instruments, dogs. Some large garden tubs were dumped on the front paving as though waiting until someone had the strength to move them through to the back. But they were never shifted; they remained where the removal men had put them. And the next summer they proved to be thickly planted with lilies, tall and lavish trumpets, arching towards the light. Extraordinary, I thought, to plant those beautiful creatures with their hint of exotic wildness in something as tame as a tub. But number nine's lilies, growing in their special peaty compost, continued to flourish after mine, planted in the clay of a London border, died out.

In a side street round the corner was a tall and undistinguished shrub growing near the footpath. In August it was suddenly covered with flowers, eye-catching single hollyhock flowers, but not in a hollyhock colour: they were beautiful blue with a plum-coloured stain in the centre, an improbable colour to encounter in that month, in that street. The shrub also turned out to have an improbable name: hibiscus. 'But hibiscus is a sub-tropical climber with orange flowers suited to the ears of Gauguin's Tahitian maidens,' I thought.

No. '*Hibiscus syriacus*,' said my book (*Effective Flowering Shrubs* by M. Haworth-Booth, 1951) 'the Bush Mallow, is a very old inhabitant of our gardens yet, although perfectly hardy, it is very rarely seen. The bush grows slowly to about [3m] 10ft in height, with upright twiggy branches and somewhat oak-like leaves.'

Across the road there grew another shrub with blue flowers which came in May. It was an evergreen, trained against a sunny wall, small and dark in leaf, small and powdery in flower. It looked vaguely familiar; but of course, I had seen it often in Australian gardens where it grew with abandon, pushed in to fight for its rights among other shrubs. I did not know its name, let alone how to pronounce it: it was ceanothus, cherished in England because of its tender nature, its need to be pampered, protected and pruned, and because its flowers are blue.

Elsewhere along the pavements the pinks and reds and yellows flamed – above all, the hybrid tea and floribunda roses. In those days the hybrid tea rose 'Peace' reigned over the suburbs, tall and healthy with huge, un-rose-like, unscented flowers of beautifully shaded colour: cowslip tinged with pink. It was succeeded (or usurped) by 'Queen Elizabeth', the even more vigorous floribunda whose debut I had seen in the horticultural hall, tall as a small tree, with unfading flowers of shrimp pink if you liked them, bubble-gum pink if you did not. In a corner garden devoted almost entirely to roses, they grew in a variety of random beds with hard stone edges, crazy beds set in crazy paving, rectangular, oval and wedge-shaped, well tended and well mulched. It was one of my stopping places; it was not to my taste, that garden much-loved by its owner, but I was trying to decide which roses these were, and which ones I liked.

Beyond it the unloved gardens extended, gardens which reproached their owners, or added to the heavy list of chores that must be faced one day, interspersed with gardens where conscientious householders had won the battle, subduing nature with concrete, replacing untidiness with spirit-cramping neatness, then positioning one or two plastic pots of red geraniums along pink concrete slabs. Which was worse, this strict, compulsive discipline, or the wilderness of sycamore seedlings and mildewed michaelmas daisy, the bits of buddleia waving dead brown cones of flowers from the mortar of cracked walls, the thickets of uncontrolled honeysuckle – mounds of dead twigs with fresh growth on the top, the dusty exhausted lavender bushes and whole walls of bindweed? And what were the guidelines for a good front garden?

'The chief function of a front garden', wrote Susan Jellicoe in *Town Gardens to Live In* (Penguin 1977), 'is to separate the house from the road and protect it from the noise and dust of traffic.'

This pronouncement, unnerving in its simplicity, was nevertheless incontestable: front gardens do separate houses from roads. The continuing existence of that well-trimmed privet hedge in the Jellicoes' front garden was now explained: wherever we live, even if we live in a Georgian terraced house, we look out on cars parked along our pavements and moving, revving, squeaking cars on the road beyond. The privet hedge hides them from view. You look out of the ground-floor window into a calm and soothing wall of green, a wall that also absorbs and deadens a little of the traffic noise.

But front gardens have a second function: they complete the architecture of the house. Here, too, the well-trimmed privet and its well-cut square of grass were right for the terraced house. Those classically inspired Grove Terrace façades with their restrained decorations of fanlight and balcony and their easy combination into a single, unified row needed no eye-catching floral distraction: the exceptional understatement of the green square of grass and hedge was not in fact 'dull' but serene. I began to think that the bulging escallonia with its piffling pink flowers next door was rather less pleasing than the privet.

Privet is cheap, vigorous and evergreen, it withstands fumes and shade, and it trims as brilliantly as box or yew or beech; you can persuade it to have sharp right-angled corners at the top; you can castellate it or train it into arches. But it must be neat. It should be trimmed four times a year. It is still there, *Ligustrum ovalifolium*, all over London, in countless residential streets. In summer it waves its unkempt, sappy growths sideways and upwards, blowsy as a woman whose figure has gone to seed, overgrown and dull, only varied by the occasional bit that is overgrown and golden, and only momentarily redeemed by the nostalgic urban scent of its flowers, like miniature sprays of cream lilac, which bloom on the tips of the untrimmed stems in summer. By late November most of it has been cut but, because of insufficient earlier pruning, it is leggy and see-through at the base.

It is not easy to enthuse about formal evergreen alternatives to the traffic-blocking, greedy, time-consuming privet screen. Halfway down our terrace, somebody embarked upon the grand and countrified idea of a yew hedge, but it was not happy in its London street. The small, expensive, inky plants sat sullenly in their generously manured border, refusing to join up with each other for years, let alone grow tall. An established holly hedge seemed to lose its sparkle here; it was impressive but forbidding, with vicious dead leaves lurking beneath it on the soil. Berberis seemed, to my eye, neither formal nor informal but an uneasy compromise between the two, with too many thorns and inadequate leaves. Hedging plants, I thought, must have leaves that agree to make a solid wall when cut. Pyracantha lost its glory, that is its fiery berries, when clipped into a hedge. Spotted laurel hovered on the verge of a fashionable comeback but subsided into impoverished obscurity. Beech and hornbeam were beautiful, but so rare that they must be difficult to establish in towns.

But round the corner from our terrace were two Victorian three-storey terraced houses where climbers instead of hedges screened the windows from parked cars. One had an anachronistic fence of horizontal white-painted slats, along which climbed the variegated ivy, *Hedera canariensis* 'Variegata'. The fence disappeared altogether beneath the abundant shields of its leaves, marbled with sage-green, grey-green and ivory. The effect was dignified and architectural, olive-dark but also ivory-bright. Nearby, on a fence made of crude steel piping, a single plant of the climbing rose 'Mermaid' grew horizontally, obliterating the metal with huge single golden flowers nestling among glossy, healthy leaves. Behind the climbers the gardens were so tiny that there was just room for the rubbish bins, and it was a single step from front window to street. But the climbers furnished the space handsomely enough, and no more was needed to complete the picture. A handful of fertiliser where the root emerged from a hole in the concrete and half-an-hour's secateur work in early spring and again in summer, and the owners could relax, well pleased.

These cottages were still part of formal terraces, where straight lines and symmetry ruled. One kilometre (half a mile) to the north, or just across the main road to the west, the street architecture changed. Here were early twentieth-century houses, where height and symmetry had gone, and so had basements, area railings, and slated roofs. There were red tiles, pebble-dash stucco mixed with brick, the easy comfort of two modest storeys, bay windows, inset porches behind brick arches and lead-lighted windows set in high-waisted front doors. The style was hybrid, and called for hybrid roses. Privet could do nothing here. A loose, informal flowering hedge can still screen the traffic from the person who sits reading or talking on the other side of the window. I had a friend who sat thus, near the bay window of a semi-detached Edwardian villa less than 2m (6ft) from the street. She loved warm colours, the colours of oriental rugs and amber beads and autumn dahlias. Her curtains were orange, and she planted a hedge of the hybrid musk rose 'Buff Beauty', so that inquisitive passers-by could look through the shaded buffs and pale oranges of the rose to the more intense colour of the curtains, but were more likely to stoop and smell the roses. Meanwhile my friend looked out, not at the pedestrians nor at the line of cars, but at her 60cm (2ft) thick, 120cm (4ft) tall, skilfully pruned and dense rose hedge.

Inspired, she planted a second rose hedge parallel to the first and growing in the narrow bed beneath the bay window. It was a hedge of the miniature rose 'Perle d'Or' (cousin of 'Cécile Brunner'), much lower than 'Buff Beauty' and more delicately shaped, but its individual tea-rose flowers were also orange, buff and cream. To complete the planting and to secure privacy, a *Cotoneaster horizontalis* grew upwards, not outwards, directly beneath the bay window, its stiff fans over the bottom 25cm (10in) of glass as effective as a net curtain and much more interesting.

Traffic-screening hedges were the exception on my walks; the low hedge was the rule: the simple dog-deterrent, the boundary marker. Grove Terrace had two excellent examples side by side, each of them arranged, with some formality, round a perfectly levelled lawn, flat and bright green as a billiard table. The first was of scarlet polyantha roses, twenty of them, not more than 45cm (18in) tall, carpeted with grape hyacinths in spring; the second was even shorter – a mere 30cm (12in) – and neater, and clipped into a rounded shape as neat as a pipe: it was *Lonicera nitida*, the favoured hedging honeysuckle with tiny leaves. Elsewhere gardeners marked their boundaries with hedges of aromatic rosemary, sorely tempting to stealing fingers, or of hardy fuchsia, luscious corollas of red and purple dangling on the shady side of a street. If these hedges did not screen the householder they heartened the passer-by.

For this is obviously a third function of a front garden: to give pleasure to other people. Front gardens are not private: most of us would shrink from sitting in our own front gardens whether there is a high hedge or not; it would be like sitting in a shop window, or on a stage. So there is no need to contrive the sense of mystery that is so desirable an element of back gardens. Instead, we want people to think 'how nice' as they walk by.

The reason I did not think 'how nice' as I passed the bright floribunda roses in the network of residential streets behind our terrace was that their colours were random. They came in blobs on the tops of their upward-reaching stems: a blob of brick red beside a blob of tangerine, a blob of yellow, a blob of pink. They were the raw materials for a picture, but a picture they were not. The pictures came with colour schemes: half-a-dozen white 'Iceberg' roses running up to a front door behind a low hedge of lavender; bright yellow roses planted in a row beside a yellow front door below a window-box of trailing, small-leafed ivy, *Hedera helix* 'Goldheart'; a square of green grass, glimpsed often from the bus, with the tall, clipped obelisk of a bay tree in the middle (a variant of the Jellicoes' garden of grass and privet), for green, as Gertrude Jekyll said, is a colour too. Here, suddenly, was a guideline: front gardens, like back gardens, can express a unifying vision.

This was why I so admired my friend's front garden: the small hedge of 'Perle d'Or' roses echoed the colours of the tall 'Buff Beauty' hedge. I had another friend with a unified front garden of larger size. It was a pattern of leaves, grey, silver and variegated: lavender and santolina bushes alternated along the path to the front door; behind them, to the left, periwinkle and variegated dead nettle (*Lamium maculatum* 'Album') carpeted a square of paving; to the right, the dull artichoke-green leaves of the plume poppy, *Macleaya cordata*, rose high in a narrow bed.

Gradually, I discovered more unified front gardens. One was a herb garden, carried out in a space 5 x 3m (15 x 9ft). Two diamond-shaped beds were set point to point in gravel and outlined neatly with Victorian edging tiles. Where the points met an urn was filled with variegated thyme; marjoram, basil, sage, santolina and feverfew filled the beds; a zigzag outer border was a mirror image of their pattern, planted with taller herbs, lovage and rose-mary.

Then there was a winter garden. It is a particularly nice idea to lift the hearts of passers-by in winter with a concentration of winter-flowering things: a whiff of mahonia or viburnum or *Daphne odora* by the gate, a glimpse of *Iris stylosa* or snowdrops by the path, the weird grey tassels of *Garrya elliptica* dangling against a garage wall, or simply the unblemished yellow stars of winter jasmine on a neatly trained plant by the front door. But this winter garden relied for its effect on foliage: round a drive in front of a detached town house was a sweeping bor-der thickly planted with dark green, bright green, blue-green, silver-grey, and pale yellow. *Skimmia japonica* was dark and rich, with clusters of tiny raspberry-pink berries; *Fatsia japonica* and *Choisya ternata* were bright, polished green; rue was blue; *Senecio greyii* was silver-grey, as grey as the half-mourning clothes of an Edwardian widow; and variegated laurel was splashed with pale yellow. Bright green looks especially fresh placed beside glaucous blue or grey. It is a sharp key-change, a sort of colour discord, but an invigorating one. The shrubs were repeated round the sweep: at midwinter the panicles of fatsia flowered high above its glossy leaves at staggered intervals all round the semi-circle; by February the white orange-blossom flowers of the choisya took over. The secret lay in repetition – and so did the unity.

And yet, when spring arrived, I lingered beside gardens where unity gave way to profusion, gardens which belonged to people who were busy fitting in as many different plants as possible. These people probably regarded studied colour schemes as mere decor – something to make the designer happy but not the horticulturalist. For them, the question about the function of front gardens was too obvious to be worth an answer: front gardens supplied a little bit of extra space to put plants in.

One day, after I had been walking up and down the terrace

for nearly twenty years, pushing prams, then pushchairs, taking children to nursery school and dancing class, exercising the dog, I noticed that an exceptional gardener had taken control at number twenty-four. I had never seen her at work; the first signal I picked up of her presence came with a low, spreading plant which seemed to be happily employed in masking the random paving with small and glossy tooth-edged leaves and rose-like flowers. Indeed, apart from its habit of growth and its miniature scale, it was exactly like a rose: 'same family', I said to myself. But it *was* a rose: 'Nozomi', recently hybridised (1968) and too good to be true; it flowered all summer, and a host of other pretty shrubs grew round it and flowered all summer too, echoing its spreading shape and pearly flowers, but setting its dark green leaves in a silver frame. There was a low and spreading rock rose, *Cistus x skanbergii*, with grey-green leaves and soft pink flowers; there was *Convolvulus cneorum* whose pink buds opened to white trumpets set among leaves of silver silk; both these were on the edge of hardiness, but this little south-west facing garden seemed warm. Lavender edged the path; behind it was a remarkable evergreen, *Ozothamnus ledifolius*, smelling of honey. Among it all there was room for a small ceanothus, *C.* 'Southmeed', and through the rose carpet grew *Aster latifolia*, a choice little daisy with sweet, tiny flowers, white and rose-Tyrian, neat as a sprigged dimity print. Beside the steps grew the cape figwort, *Phygelius capensis*, offsetting the soft pastels of the garden with lush green leaves like a fuchsia's and dangling orange bugle flowers. There was no strict colour scheme here, yet the little garden did not lack a sense of unity: it was a sense of something warm, sun-loving and aromatic. It was to be ten more years before I met its gardener (see Plate 1).

Meanwhile, something was happening in our own front garden. Eileen had returned. Widowed for the second time, she came back to live in the basement flat. She had given us the house; now we were going to give her back a little bit of house and garden. So we excavated the basement area. Down came the area railings, away went the huge old coal cellars, away went the tiny border of miniature roses and the bigger border of hybrid teas (good riddance). A sloping path and a few shallow steps led gently down to a new paved courtyard on the old basement level; a new sash window reached from ceiling to floor with a new wooden window-box specially built to go across its base, and a new square bed was constructed against a retaining wall facing back towards the window.

But the soil was old. Among all the excavation, the topsoil had disappeared and the stuff the builders shovelled back into the bed was sticky as toffee and dank as the coal cellars which had so recently occupied the space. We had paid for York paving slabs, but foolishly, we did not pay for a load of new soil, thinking that the old topsoil would re-emerge.

I shook an old *Fatsia japonica* out of its indoor flowerpot and stuck it in this sticky bed to supply a background of evergreen leafage for delectable plants to be chosen later. The courageous fatsia never looked back. It looked upwards and outwards, absolutely indifferent to its sickly soil; outwards went its great eight-fingered palmate leaves, the picture of polished health, and upwards grew its mighty panicles of ivory flowerheads high above the brick retaining wall; glad to be out of its pot, it vied with the magnolia for dominance in our front garden. So I learnt one thing: if you have a really nasty, dark, cheerless bit of London soil, *Fatsia japonica* will grow there. Indeed, it will probably prefer it to the richest compost in a root-restricting tub. Tubs were for choicer things – camellias, for instance.

We planted camellias in big half-barrels on the new basement paving. Success was instant. No disgusting old soil for them – they had brand new bags of peat mixed with John Innes compost No. 3. As their roots are in balls lying not far below the surface, they were unaware of being cramped in tubs. In earliest spring the unbelievable waxy pink single flowers of *Camellia x williamsii* 'J.C. Williams' smothered the plant and defied wintry February (for this low paving was sheltered from wind and shaded from the danger of early-morning sun on top of overnight frost, and thus ideal for camellia flowers). All year round the glossy, dark camellia leaves stood handsomely against the biscuit colour of London stock bricks, and when the flowers were over, they did not linger damply brown on the branches, but dropped politely to the ground.

I applied a lesson learnt from other people's front gardens and planted lilies, three 'jumbo' bulbs of *Lilium regale*, in a flowerpot. They bloomed abundantly, their heavy scent drifting upwards to enrapture people standing on the front doorsteps, unaware that there were lilies blooming in a pot 3m (10ft) below.

Eileen had long yellow velvet curtains at her new long window. She wanted yellow roses, not to create a front garden colour scheme, but to cut for her dining table. In went two 'Allgolds' in square brown plastic tubs (chosen for their modest price). They were a sad disappointment, looking gawky and flowering sparsely, as though they did not share the camellias' attitude to root-restricting life in a tub.

She chose a beautiful large-bloomed repeat-flowering clematis for her north-facing wall, the sort that needs little or no pruning: *Clematis patens* 'The President'. It was planted in the dank shade of the bed in the belief that its love of a cool root-run would make it flourish there. For two years it did, spreading its large and lovely purple-claret flowers along the wall. A few more plantings like this, we thought, and the basement garden will really be quite pretty. But we never found the things we should have planted in that square bed: variegated ivy or periwinkle to trail over its retaining wall in front, hardy fuchsias to dangle above, and arching ferns; pale striped grasses like gardener's garters (*Phalaris arundinacea* 'Picta'), and perhaps *Hydrangea sargentiana* with its huge dull felted leaves to tower at the back. We were depressed with it before we had given it a fair try. Since then, I have looked down with admiration into dark and narrow basements – far more difficult than ours – which have been made into arbours of leafiness simply by planting thickly with tolerant bright evergreens (the familiar roll-call of fatsia, choisya and skimmia) or with the sharp brilliance of the wreathing golden hop (*Humulus lupulus* 'Aureus'), interspersed with pale flowers like the white bleeding heart (*Dicentra spectabilis* 'Alba') and white lobelia.

Eileen went away, back to Australia. Subsequently, a fleeting tenant of the basement flat who was also a gardener and a friend planted in the bed an *Acer palmatum* 'Atropurpureum', an outstanding Japanese maple with fine-cut leaves that are less purple than claret; in autumn it is incandescent when the light shines through it. Fresh from the nursery and liberally furnished with peat, it looked a young aristocrat. But our friend moved on and a succession of tenants moved in and out; the maple discovered the truth about the soil in its bed and began to repine. We shifted it to a large pot, having heard that Japanese maples make flourishing tub plants, and stood it on the upper level at the feet of the magnolia where, in spirit, it belonged. At once it responded and became healthy and elegant again.

People move on. This is the trouble with gardens, and particularly with gardens in big cities where tall houses are subdivided into flats, where people are packed in tightly and leases pass from hand to hand. Someone takes over a front garden and some hopeful plants appear; then the place changes hands and precious scraps of white perennial wallflower and leggy euphorbia struggle to survive among colonies of willow-herb; or some trendy variegated dead nettle, intended for a strict square yard of carpeting, romps unrestrained over the whole area, suffocating weaker things, while the outgoing leaseholder embarks upon an imaginative garden elsewhere.

When the time came for our second daughter to move away from home I joined the restless flat-hunt. In the evenings we drove the streets together; in the daytimes I drove alone, rather enjoying the chase. It brought to me a realisation of a

front garden's fourth possible function: to beautify its street
by giving it a climber or a tree. Who wants a flat in a treeless
street?

Our councils work hard to soften our urban vistas with
foliage. Once they planted huge trees, not only the inimitable
plane but the lime, deliciously scented but dropping stickiness on
the roofs of cars – you still see them severely pollarded in rows
along nineteenth-century residential streets. Now the councils
plant slim-line trees: rowans, the ferny-leafed 'mountain ash'
(*Sorbus vilmorinii* or *S. discolor*), flowering in spring, fruiting
in autumn, colouring brilliantly but keeping within bounds; the
related whitebeam, *Sorbus aria* (Gerard Manley Hopkins called
it 'windbeat Whitebeam' when comparing it to the Milky Way)
whose leaves are felted with silver, more intense when they turn
to show their undersides in the wind; and the graceful silver
birches which have the knack of looking right wherever they
are placed, never too wide, never too tall, never less than shapely
because of the way they carry their small leaves dangling downwards, because of their autumn colour of molten gold lasting
long after most brilliant reds have fallen, and because of their
shining white, blotched stems. They adorn all frontages in all
weathers.

Householders don't always follow the example of these
prudent professional plantings but hopefully cram favourite
spreading trees into tiny spaces. I used to pass a weeping
willow, whose ultimate span is 15m (50ft), squashed into the
corner of a front garden beside the rubbish bin in a space 2m
(6ft) square. But I also passed the fashionable new front-garden
trees which have superseded the lilac and laburnum of our
grandparents. For tiny spaces there was a tiny willow: *Salix
caprea* 'Kilmarnock', weeping in bell-shaped neatness, covered
with catkins and only 2.7m (9ft) tall; for wider sites there was
the silvery willow-leafed pear, *Pyrus salicifolia* 'Pendula', more
interested in spreading and weeping than in growing tall; the
favourite was the golden false acacia, *Robinia pseudoacacia*

'Frisia', fast-growing and slender, its leaves of an improbable sharp lemon-green which makes springtime seem to last right through dull August days. My own booby prize went to *Eucalyptus gunnii*, many people's favourite for its height, speed of growth, slender habit and blue-grey evergreen leaves. To my Australian eyes it looked a laughing stock, a forest tree transplanted to a city street where it must lean outwards at a rakish angle from the shadow of its house as if searching for the wide, dry, bright landscape of Australia where it belonged.

My favourites were the flowering fruit trees, the Japanese cherries, crab apples and plums which, when they bloom in spring, make city streets seem lovely places. But the spreading cherries need room, and the favoured upward-branching one, 'Kanzan', has an unfortunate shape like an umbrella blown inside-out and young bronze leaves which clash with its opulent sprays of sugar-pink flowers. Crab apples are smaller and shapelier; *Malus* 'Golden Hornet' is spectacular in November, its fruit hanging like a foretaste of Christmas decorations, golden balls on bare branches when the leaves have fallen. The crab apples and plums with deep red or purple leaves, glimpsed from a passing car, give a sense of shade and depth to the middle distance of a street.

Tall climbers give a street a different sort of beauty. Many terraced houses have nowhere to plant a tree, no front garden but only a basement, but from dark beds or barrels in these basements every now and then flowering climbers rise. They mount in panels of green up three or four storeys, swarming up drainpipes, demarcating one terraced house from the next, and bringing leafiness to dull façades. Sometimes it is honeysuckle; often it is *Polygonum baldschuanicum*, the mile-a-minute Russian vine, softening all available edges from ground to rooftop with billowing clouds of creamy flowers; on a lucky day it is wisteria. I visited a street where two houses had planted wisteria. One was in full flower, relaxed and prodigal, the voluptuous mauve racemes falling over each other in tiers like dangling bunches of grapes, each tapering raceme seeming held in suspension between the pull of gravity and attachment to the branch. But the wisteria a few yards down the road was not flowering at all.

There were other people, like me, who had planted rampant roses on their house-fronts. The loveliest was *Rosa banksiae* 'Lutea', festooning a warm frontage with sprays of tiny flowers as pale as primroses in May; the easiest was 'Golden Showers', planted beside a north-facing porch and content to make a pretty pillar not too wide and not too tall.

One evening we rounded a corner in Kentish Town and saw a rambling rose in full flower, so floriferous and wide-spreading that its dingy surroundings did not signify. Its leaves were shiny, its young shoots copper-coloured, its buds warm salmon, it opened pale flesh pink. Briefly we believed that this must be the street where our hunt would end – the street of the perfect flat. Disappointingly, it was not. But we identified the rose; it was the old favourite rambler 'Albertine'.

Weeks later my daughter, near despair, settled for what she thought was a distinctly imperfect flat on the ground floor, with responsibility for a sizeable front garden. There was a large square of concrete paving slabs on which sat two generous old tubs, sawn-in-half beer barrels, full of chickweed and used by the local cats as litter-boxes. (Someone had once grown tulips there – we saw their remains in a few feeble furls of leaf.) More chickweed and dandelions grew between the paving slabs and there was rubbish everywhere: crisp wrappers, crumpled newspaper, plastic bottles, blown up the path to lie among a bank of old brown plane-tree leaves under the front step. The hedge was not quite high enough to give privacy to the bedroom window which faced this way: it was the familiar *Berberis darwinii*, very prickly and not especially distinguished, but prepared to colour well in autumn. Along the boundary between this property and the next soared the even more familiar unclipped privet. The house itself was part of a nineteenth-century terrace, its woodwork was

white, its stucco and bricks colour-washed a sort of mulberry
or plum. White with touches of pale blue seemed a good colour
scheme for the front garden. My daughter cheerfully endured
parental prodding, and planted a combination of tulips that I
admire: 'White Triumphator' and black 'Queen of the Night',
underplanted with forget-me-nots for spring. It was a partial
failure: the local cats enjoyed the refurbished compost in the
tubs, scratching holes in the surface and disturbing the bulbs
(we fought back with little bits of thorny berberis, cut from the
hedge and stuck into the tubs at 15cm (6in) intervals). When the
surviving tulips flowered, the local children picked them. But in
summer there were frilly white petunias interspersed with pale
blue lobelia. People don't pick petunias or lobelia, and the berberis twigs, though hidden, were still there, so the cats didn't
come and the planting worked. Tall white geraniums grew in
a new window-box as an outdoor curtain for the bedroom,
with bits of variegated ivy, transplanted from the back garden,
trailing at each end.

But what about a tree, to give further privacy outside the
window and pleasure to passers-by, pedestrians and motorists
alike? It was a matter of heaving up four concrete slabs in
the centre of the paving, and enriching the deprived earth
underneath with peat and bonemeal and whatever else seemed
likely at the local garden centre. The little bed was ready for
the prettiest crab apple we had seen on our rounds: *Malus
floribunda*, of modest size and weeping habit, but prodigal
with April blossom, red in bud, pink on first opening, white
when full-blown. In flower it could scarcely be more charming.
In leaf it was green (wine-red against that plum façade would
not have done).

'We're planting a tree,' we said brightly, spades under
insteps, when the upstairs tenant came down the path.

'A *tree*!' she echoed, anxious, incredulous, fearing the worst.

The worst, for us, nearly happened. Some house painters
mutilated the young branches with their ladders, and it was a

case of desperate pruning back. The little tree did not seem to falter; it put out more vigorous new weeping growths, and set about its task of furnishing the front garden.

We dug one more hole, in the angle between the berberis and privet hedges. Here we planted a rambler rose, to lie along the berberis, using it as a capacious bolster on which to sprawl and stretch, and adding to its modest height an exuberant 30cm (1ft) or so. This was my daughter's present to the neighbourhood. Her street was called Albert Street; her rose was 'Albertine'.

VII

In a Sunny Courtyard

Water your damned flower-pots, do!

Robert Browning, 'Soliloquy of the Spanish Cloister'

The French windows were triply invisible: first came a burglar grid, then full and nicotine-tinted nylon curtains, then thick oatmeal curtains. But if you pulled the curtain cord, shouldered back the nylon, wrenched the burglar grid back along its rails and found the right key, you could unlock the metal-framed French door and step out into a small, square garden. This was the back of the Albert Street flat.

It was 3.6 x 4.4m (12 x 14ft 6in). Its walls were brick, with the remains of whitewash on them. It was paved in concrete blocks, and across the far wall and along half of one of the flanks was a raised bed with a brick retaining wall. So far, so good: raised beds are the things to go for in small town gardens, since they give an extra depth of soil which in theory can be good loam, not London clay, and they lift the flowers to eye-level, so that in an outdoor room the flowers serve as pictures on a wall. Concrete blocks may not be as nice as York stone or brick, but are better than concrete screed, and these were an unassuming grey, which we preferred to pink.

But the touch that singled out this garden came at its corner: instead of turning at right-angles, the raised bed rounded the corner with a scooped-out, concave curve, and into this curve fitted a small round bed at ground level with an edging of bricks. Bricks redeemed the concrete slabs. Clearly this garden had once had ambitions: a designer had been at work.

Now, bindweed ruled, the large-leafed bindweed with white trumpet flowers (*Calystegia sepium*), and it wreathed the borders from side to side and back to front. It curtained a tall and vigorous forsythia, it festooned a toppling *Cotoneaster horizontalis* whose branches were fanning right out over the paving and shading the little round bed from view, though once it had clearly been intended as a wall shrub (the wall nails were still there, their patent lead loops now drooping and restraining nothing). Among the bindweed two sumptuous red and purple fuchsias were dangling, and beneath it some surly *Sedum spectabile* was hanging on to life. A rampant white jasmine grew up the house in a flourishing column from a corner by the windows, and an avocado pear was sprouting from a stone pushed into the edge of the raised bed – a memento, surely, of happier times in the garden.

'This is marvellous!' I said.

Dead silence from my daughter.

'This is good,' I faltered. 'You could plant herbs in that little bed,' I said.

By now I had the instant confidence of seasoned gardeners; at least I knew enough to be emphatically opinionated. I stepped out into the small space and saw at once what could (should) be planted there.

The garden caught the sun. The terraced house lay to the north-east; there were no near buildings to the south or west, only the remains of long gardens beyond the walls. The backs of the houses in the adjoining street were 30m (100ft) away. Delicious smells of lunch, spicy, Italian or Greek, drifted from next door. I saw the garden as a green and aromatic oasis supplying

PLATE 5   *A new garden in Highgate waits for white roses to climb its hand-made trellises and for edging plants to soften its brick and stone paving.*

my daughter with everything she might need for flavouring her cooking. Tactfully and sensibly, she acquiesced.

I stood on a chair and repainted the outside walls white. First, I put on a primer to hold the patches of damp green at bay. Then I brushed Snowcem over the rough and pock-marked surfaces. It never occurred to me not to repaint the bricks, nor to paint them a different colour. I *knew* that white was nice. I had not yet met the school of thought which teaches that white brings the background to the foreground, reducing apparent size.

There was a white metal garden table with a cracked and filthy plate-glass top pushed into a corner, and beside it a two-seater white metal bench and an uncomfortable little curly white chair. The white was plastic coating welded on to metal and beginning to crack off. Patches of rust were coming through. Upside down beneath the forsythia and camouflaged with bindweed we found a second chair.

'I don't like them,' said my daughter.

'But they're terribly expensive to buy new and they're not half bad,' I said, worried lest she undervalue the find. 'They only need painting.'

I did not offer to do the painting, they were so exhaustingly twirled and spiralled. She did it herself, anointing every curlicue with a special anti-rust solution before applying white gloss. We got a new sheet of glass cut; a skilful friend made beautifully fitting cushions out of foam cut to precisely the right size – a rectangle for the bench and two circles for the chairs, covered in fresh bitter green and white print, with piping. Rearranged together against one of the white-washed walls, this garden suite had undeniable chic.

The forsythia was not so chic, however. I was a sufficient gardening snob by now to know it was positively dowdy. It took

PLATE 6 *The small and square backyard becomes a bower of container plants regularly rearranged by their owner Thomasina Tarling.*

up the best position in the garden, the end of the border nearest to the house. It should be scrapped and replaced by something rarer: there was enough forsythia in other people's gardens to satisfy any need for yellow blossom at forsythia-flowering time. Yet I was reluctant to pass on this sort of gardener's intolerance to my daughter. Besides, it would be ungrateful to the cheery forsythia, which might look bright and fairly beautiful in spring.

The *Cotoneaster horizontalis* I now recognised as less than thrilling, too, but I had a lingering loyalty to the plant that had impressed me long ago in Sir Frederick Gibberd's front garden, so I contented myself with sternly pruning it and pinning it back against the wall, where it looked instantly architectural again. I dug out the bindweed; to my astonishment, it was less tenacious than its small-leafed cousin, and did not reappear. I scattered bonemeal on the soil (fairly nasty soil it proved to be, of course, all stones and clay) and forked in such compost as we could muster. I persuaded my daughter that she must have a mock orange to scent her whole garden in July. There was just room for one at the other end of the border, near the seat; we bought a small one, *Philadelphus* 'Sybille', with single flowers and weeping habit. It was to weep over the retaining wall.

I carried two sawn-in-half barrels through the flat and painted them in the old, tried formula: glossy white wood with black iron bands. It was clear to me that tubs and pots were needed if the garden was to form a leafy picture. Satisfactory as the raised beds were, they offered very little planting space. And all those plants that thrive in containers were clamouring for inclusion: a camellia, a bay tree, regale lilies, a fig.

The maker of the cushions had a garden where figs seeded themselves everywhere. She dug one up, a mere 23cm (9in) seedling, and it settled down perfectly and started to grow. I felt sure it would behave well in a tub. It needed root restriction.

A camellia was indispensable: ravishing, tub-tolerant, winter-flowering, evergreen. We bought the famous 'Donation'; it is no more beautiful than my 'J.C. Williams', rather less refined, if anything, but it is easier to come by. You could buy it fairly cheaply at about 30cm (12in) tall. It, too, settled down at once, looked right, and began to grow.

Humbler, but obviously suitable, was a bay tree; you see them growing happily in cramped containers everywhere. Trimmed and trendy in house-and-garden centres, they cost a lot, but a rooted cutting from a country nursery cost a pound or two and in a small earthenware pot it did not look ridiculous, and it had leaves to spare for stews from the start.

We filled another pot with regale lilies. I was rolling out 'a few of my favourite things' – but why deny oneself the scent of lilies in a little garden which is in need of plants in pots? The pots, in varying sizes from large to small, from tall to wide, were to stand in groups against the walls. They could be moved, like furniture, into prominence or obscurity according to the season. When the lilies finished flowering, they could be pushed into a corner, to be succeeded in August by a large pot of white agapanthus – another prize container plant – and by the dangling bells of *Galtonia candicans*, the summer hyacinth. We agreed that white flowers should dominate the garden: best of all with green leaves and white furniture, and best of all at night, when returning workers step outside to breathe: philadelphus, regale lilies, jasmine and tobacco flowers – all white, all luminous in the dark.

We went together to an RHS fortnightly show and saw a display of conservatory plants, among them a little lemon tree with two full-sized lemons on it. She loved it and I bought it for her. Who cares what may happen in winter, I thought. It is irresistible *now*.

At a garden centre my daughter pointed out a handsome, glossy climber beginning its journey up a bamboo stake. It had the special luxuriance of an indoor plant, and proved to be the half-hardy fatshedera, bright green and polished like a fatsia, but climbing like an ivy – a lovely cross between two parent plants. In this warm and sheltered garden it had a good chance of survival. We bought it, together with a large pot to plant it in. Though not self-clinging, it could be held to the wall with patent nails and trained to make a bright evergreen garland above the white iron seat.

Fatshedera, bay tree, camellia — these would look after the winter scene. It would be sad to look out through big windows in December and see no leaves at all. By February, small terracotta troughs along the concrete window-sill could be thickly flowering with early bulbs: the intense blue dwarf *Iris histrioides* interspersed with the buttery-cream of *Crocus chrysanthus* 'Cream Beauty'. They would seem to be growing at your feet as you sat in the warmth on the other side of the glass. A little later there could be *Iris reticulata* 'Cantab' and miniature narcissi 'Jack Snipe' and 'Tête-à-tête', with two little trumpets on a single stem. The bulbs were not expensive when bought in window-box quantities; they could be regarded as expendable and replaced with bedding plants in summer.

All this was there, half-realised in my inward eye, from the beginning. It was not to be primarily a flower garden; the idea was leafiness. Peaceful and sunny as it was, it only needed shapely leaves against the white brick walls. In short, it needed a grape vine.

I bought one, *Vitis vinifera* 'Brant', at an autumn flower show in Vincent Square. It, too, was irresistible, its leaves already turned to ruby. We planted it in the border opposite the window, so that it could be trained along the wall and round the corner to climb the adjoining south-facing wall. When my daughter drew back her curtains the morning after we had planted it and saw it flaming against the whitewash she experienced the joy of garden ownership. 'My vine,' she said over the telephone, 'is *beautiful*!'

She was pleased with her garden, and became skilled at the sort of bedding-out needed in a very small courtyard full of pots. She would go to the garden centre and return with white petunias, which she liked, and scented white tobacco plants (*Nicotiana alata*) which she loved. She would buy new herbs each spring after mysterious dwindlings and disappearances of last year's tarragon and parsley, rosemary and chives. Each year the round herb bed would be replenished: five or six little plants would spread out quickly to fill the bed in a single summer. There were lavender, purple-leafed sage, creeping thyme, giant chives and bright green basil. Sometimes the basil seedlings would be planted out in the pots vacated by the early bulbs.

She worked with speed and accuracy, clutching her scarlet trowel. She had a keen eye for pests – little insects on young shoots, snails beneath flower pots – and angrily sprayed the aphids and sprinkled turquoise-blue slug pellets round the garden in spring.

She also tended to be angry with the plants that faltered.

'Something's the matter with my bloody fatshedera!' she said when its leaves started turning a bilious yellow. 'I think it's dying.'

But she concealed her anger if she caught me grimly testing the dryness of the potting compost with my finger when I thought she wasn't looking.

Our recurrent gardening exchange went as follows:

ME: You must water every day in summer, specially the things in pots, whether it rains or not. Things in borders can get their roots down to the damp but things in pots can't.
SHE: I *have* watered!

Watering was indeed a difficulty. There was no outside tap. You had to fill the cumbersome green watering-can (left behind by the previous owner) at the kitchen sink, where it barely fitted under the tap, and then stagger across the carpet with it, trying not to spill it. If you were to water all the tubs and pots adequately you needed to fill it nine or ten times – an almost intolerable bore. The rose of the can was badly designed and the water fanned out too widely, but when you knocked the rose off water rushed out too quickly and ran straight through the pots and out on to the paving. ('You *must* keep the rose on the can,' I said.) Watering the big tubs in the front garden was worse; you had to fight your way through the front door of the flat, which would not stay open unless propped, across the pale tiles of the entrance hall, spilling water as you went, and through the main front door of the house which had two different locks and did not want to stay open either.

Garden rubbish was another problem. If the little courtyard was to look its best it must be repeatedly swept like a room – it *was* an outdoor room. The empty snail-shells, the dry twigs, the dead leaves, and my occasional prunings and dead-headings and intermittent weedings must all be packed into plastic sacks and carted through the flat and through the two heavy doors to join the latest collection of windblown litter from the street in front. And where should the bags of garden rubbish finally go? Surreptitiously into other people's skips? Or away in the boot of the car?

Despite these problems, the garden prospered. The fig grew into a little tree and produced green figs. The bay tree grew fast, and had to be potted on, and on. It sent up a tall and vigorous stem with a tuft of leaves on top, asking to be turned into a clipped ball on a smart standard. This was easily done, it was simply a matter of pruning off all side growths and allowing the top to grow until it reached the circumference of an imagined circle where it was restrained by secateurs.

The camellia grew, stately, shapely, 1.5m (5ft) tall, and never failed to flower in its due season, from February almost to May.

The fatshedera recovered from its indisposition and spread out to left and right, its leaves like exquisite small replicas of the fatsia's palmate shape, but at the same time clear-cut like ivy leaves against the white wall, though brighter and more shining.

The paved courtyard with a circular herb bed.

1 Cotoneaster horizontalis   4 fig
2 vine   5 Japanese maple
3 table and chairs   6 camellia

The lemon was moved indoors in cold spells, and put up robustly with the sharp change from cold air to central heating. It did not actually make any more lemons, but that was because it was broken in two by a heavy object dropping on it from above in a high wind. But it clung on to life, and made a new shoot.

The avocado we replanted in a pot where it was doing altogether too well and growing ridiculously tall until it too, was broken in the wind.

The grape vine encircled the garden, irrepressibly vigorous despite twice-yearly pruning in February and July, and by August there were plentiful bunches of dangling grapes half-hidden behind leaves.

And my daughter got a strong friend to dig up her forsythia. We went to buy a rose to take its place, for how can you have a garden without a single rose in it? We were after an old-fashioned shrub, but when we got home we found our plant had a label saying 'Carefree Beauty' attached just above its graft, disagreeing with the labelling at the garden centre. By then we had planted it and lacked the grim singleness of purpose to dig it up again. If it was called 'Carefree Beauty' the odds were that it would prove a charming and insouciant interloper adding a joky touch of piquancy to the garden. Not a bit of it: it was a bright pink, scentless floribunda – a nonentity, though healthy and willing. We still hadn't the heart to dig it up. Instead, I advised a second floribunda rose to be planted beside it, between it and the window: the indomitable 'Iceberg', I thought, could be relied upon to flower all summer long and would correct the floppy pinkness of 'Carefree Beauty' with its pure white flowers. A bit of *Alchemilla mollis* in front of 'Iceberg' would hide its gawky stems. And thus it was that greenfly, black spot and mildew all moved in to the warm, enclosed and largely birdless garden.

Three years later we sold our Grove Terrace house. All our children had now moved out; it was too big for us, too expensive. We moved to a flat with a communal garden looked after by another tenant, and removal men carried two heavy pots, one with the Japanese maple, the other with *Daphne odora* 'Aureomarginata', to continue their lives in Albert Street along with another pot of regale lilies. My daughter gave me a bunch of keys and invited me to potter about in her courtyard whenever I felt a longing for a bit of London earth. I became her official gardener instead of her unofficial meddler. At weekends I was happy in our Norfolk cottage garden, where I had now been busy through years of school holidays. On weekdays, when the sun shone, I occasionally let myself into Albert Street, frowning anxiously, intent on sniffing out trouble. I discovered white infestations on the bay tree's stem, sooty black deposits on its leaves: scale insects! I dabbed and rubbed with methylated spirit on cotton wool until they disappeared and the leaves shone again. I found moss stealthily advancing over the brick edging of the herb bed and began to scrape it away with a spade, feeling guilty because my daughter loved moss. The vine had flung a long arm out over the wall and was giving its most generous effects to a next-door neighbour; I stood precariously on tiptoe on the raised bed and lassooed it back again. The cotoneaster was once more threatening to engulf the garden, spreading a low parasol over the herb bed; the poor 'Iceberg' rose was trying to grow up behind it, covered with young aphids and incipient mildew in its dark and airless spot. The jasmine was layering itself into the fig tree's tub. I no longer had a problem over what to snip with my secateurs.

I played with colours and shapes in the little herb bed, putting a bit of golden marjoram beside blue rue, and trying some disproportionately tall herbs, bronze fennel and angelica, in the middle. I could also experiment with other people's ideas. At a Chelsea Show Beth Chatto had placed a verbascum in a pot as a strong accent in an otherwise soft and lyrical display. Pots are usually filled with plants that weep or spill or spread; it was inspiring to see instead a strong stem soaring up from the squat container, its basal rosette of leaves exactly filling the pot's circumference. I copied her idea, buying a healthy *Verbascum x hybridum* 'Gainsborough' at a garden centre, and standing it in a pot by the herb bed and waiting for it to grow. 'Gainsborough' is the palest cowslip colour, not particularly in tune with the original vision of Mediterranean warmth and white flowers, more evocative of English herbaceous borders and cottage gardens.

But the clarity of that first vision was dissolving. Other visions dropped over it, like successive images in a magic lantern. Why did I feel so sure that the round bed was right for herbs? Would it not have been equally right for a little tree? Would not most herbs thrive rather better in special compost in clean pots than in that dank and pebbly clay? Or if a tree in the bed would have threatened the suntrap with shade, could not a tree have been planted in the raised bed where the forsythia had been, in preference to roses? The exquisite winter-flowering cherry (*Prunus subhirtella* 'Autumnalis') of course would have given the rapture of its blossom across the plate-glass window in winter, and in summer its branches would have reached out across the garden so that you could not see, from indoors, exactly what lay beyond, and in this way the garden would have seemed bigger.

But I did not know, when we first stepped out into that small space, that expert gardeners can conjure an illusion of mystery inside a pocket handkerchief.

VIII

The Small and Square

I have a garden of my own
But so with roses overgrown
And lilies, that you would it guess
To be a little wilderness . . .

Andrew Marvell 'The Nymph
Complaining of the death of her Faun'

Once upon a time they were backyards, those spaces 5m (15ft) square behind the terraced cottages of nineteenth-century urban streets. They were not quite square, for into them there usually jutted a privy with an outside door – the single-storey extension which has now become a bathroom, kitchen or utility room in modern conversions of workmen's cottages. The yards were full of junk as well as rubbish bins: old bicycle wheels, old washtubs, old scrubbing boards, old timber. Often they were cluttered with extra extensions, ramshackle sheds and rabbit hutches. In some there might be a valiant attempt to grow food. (Mr Pooter at 'The Laurels', Brickfield Terrace, Holloway, waited for mustard and cress and radishes to sprout in his back garden, but then he was quite superior, with an altogether larger garden running down to the railway line.) The true backyards quickly degenerated into slums, infinitely grimy, filmed with smoke from a thousand domestic chimneys, described by Dickens as exhibiting 'every stage of dilapidated blind and curtain, crippled flowerpot, cracked glass, dusty decay, and miserable makeshift.' Occasionally the crippled flowerpot would hold a brave chrysanthemum, but more often the chrysanthemum lived on a window-sill indoors, and the function of the backyard, apart from housing junk, was to dry the washing. Above the grime, washing flapped on zigzags of washing lines everywhere and was sometimes even spread on the ground. Today these slums have gone, and the little terraced houses are much prized. The washing tumbles in electric driers, and the backyards have become bowers.

In the years since I first helped my daughter with her garden I have got to know three such bowers. They are all inward-looking. Nothing seems to beckon beyond their boundaries so each is saying: 'Look at *me*! Don't look beyond, there's no need to look further than *me*!' They are self-contained capsules of created beauty held within walls, fence panels or trellis. Each belongs to a woman who has found herself, because of divorce, or widowhood, or children leaving home, starting all over again with a new small garden.

The first, in Richmond, Surrey, was a rather deadly area of dull pink concrete blocks measuring 5.5m (18ft) square, when Ann, its new owner, arrived. Round its two sunless walls ran a crampingly narrow raised bed faced with bricks. Along the sunny side was a mere edging of earth between paving and boundary wall. There were two climbing roses in the shade: 'Paul's Scarlet Climber', whose vivid sprays of semi-double flowers Ann particularly disliked, was fighting for its rights against a powerful, prickly sucker; the other, at right angles to it, was 'Zéphirine Drouhin', suffused in mildew and black spot, but still producing enough intense, cerise-pink flowers to clash with its scarlet neighbour. The inevitable 'Queen Elizabeth' floribunda was a freestanding specimen in one of the beds, along with 'a nasty kerria'. There were three clematis: *C. montana* 'Rubens', doing splendidly across the back wall of the house, with cool pink flowers; 'Nellie Moser', producing her familiar pale mauve with carmine stripes on the opposite wall; and the rich crimson 'Ville de Lyons' flowering in a corner. Thus almost everything in the garden, from paving to eaves, belonged in the pink, puce, scarlet, crimson section of the spectrum.

Ann had lived for twenty years in another house in Richmond, with a beautiful garden where she and her husband had grown a flourishing pomegranate tree. Now her husband was dead, which was why she was moving here. She was going to try and grow a miniature pomegranate (*Punica granatum* 'Nana') in the warmest corner. She could not embark on any major restructuring schemes; she could not widen the raised beds or scrap the pink concrete slabs and start again. She devised a minimum of change for maximum effect.

She pulled out 'Paul's Scarlet' but left its sucker, which she hoped would be a pale, single, wild rose, and she trained it beautifully against the white-painted brick wall. She had nine slabs of pink concrete lifted, slightly off-centre, and the resultant square of ground was repaved in London stock bricks laid in a basket pattern. A square of seemly brick paving can redeem a wilderness of concrete blocks. Between the bricks were chinks where small plants could grow.

Beyond the brick square she decided to place a pot, the biggest pot she could find in the garden centre. In it she would grow a small tree, so that at a single stroke the squareness of her garden would be broken; there would be something to arrest the eye halfway across the space, and a sense of further space beyond.

She made one other major purchase: she bought three arches. Arches are beautiful in their own right provided, she thought, that they are real arches, not angular or pointed with rustic pitched roofs, but rounded at the top. She found some in a garden sundries catalogue and ordered two medium-sized 1m x 2m (3ft 6in x 7ft 6in), and one jumbo 1.7m (5ft 6in) wide and over 2.4m (8ft) high. The big one was placed by itself against the wall facing south; the other two stood side by side, facing the house. She would resist the temptation to cover them with roses, for roses demand more strenuous attention, pruning and spraying than she might be able to give as the years went by.

Clematis arches, a square of brick paving and a eucalypt in a large pot give style to this small backyard.

She removed 'Zéphirine Drouhin' with a slight pang of guilt; but not only was it sick, it conflicted with a colour scheme that was forming in her mind. She would cover her arches with clematis, not pink, nor red, nor striped, but blue and white.

Blue and white was to be Ann's colour scheme. A colour scheme, she felt, would be a challenge; its discipline might unify her tiny plot and prevent patchiness; it would usefully limit her choice, making the task of choosing between all the flowers she loved a little easier.

She determined to be quite strict in the carrying-out of

her plan. *Blue* was what she was after, not lavender or mauve. She wrote to Blackmore and Langdon, monarchs of the delphinium, enclosing small painted colour-patterns of acceptable blues, and asking for suggested varieties to match them. They readily replied with a choice of four possibilities: 'Skyline', 'Fenella,' 'Crystella' and 'Blue Nile'. They soared up into flower next year, majestic delphinium spikes of luminous cerulean blue or sapphire, one with a white and one with a black eye.

She wrote to Fisks of Westleton, the clematis growers, enclosing careful paintings of the three clematis she had inherited so that at least she might know their names, for she would not eliminate them until their substitutes had grown, and again asking for recommendations of clematis in white and blue. They attached names to her paintings with no difficulty, and recommended *C. macropetela*, *C. alpina* 'Frances Rivis', *C.* x 'Perle d'Azur', all in shades of blue, and *C.* x 'Marie Boisellot' in white.

So she planted her clematis, in blue and white, at the feet of her three arches, and white honeysuckle behind the two smaller arches as stop-gaps to serve until the clematis had grown. She planted two scented shrubs with white flowers: a philadelphus for the shadiest corner in the angle of the raised beds (because of the corner's darkness, she chose *Philadelphus coronarius* 'Aureus' which has clear lime-green young leaves in spring) and on the other side, near the delphiniums, *Viburnum x carlcephalum*, whose flowers in May are luxuriant white globes of scent.

For spring her colour scheme would be easy. There is no shortage of tiny, early bulbs in blue or white to choose from: snowdrops, pale blue crocuses, ultramarine chionodoxas and scillas, powder-blue dwarf irises and grape hyacinths, white cyclamen. In April the starry blue *Anemone blanda* might seed itself in shady places among blue hepatica, followed by forget-me-nots. There would be pulmonaria in its least pink, most blue mood; lithospermum, spreading its small dark leaves and cobalt-blue flowers over the brick edging along with periwinkle (*Vinca minor*), and *Brunnera macrophylla* 'Variegata' with its intensely blue forget-me-not-like flowers above cream-blotched, heart-shaped leaves. Almost all the raised shady border could be carpeted in early spring flowers, white and blue. But there must be room for a few clumps of summer flowers: *Meconopsis betonicifolia*, the shade-loving poppy with the fragile blue flower; green-and-white pincushions of astrantia, blue penstemons, white foxgloves, smoke-blue globe thistles (*Echinops ritro*) and bright blue *Salvia patens*. And of course there would be shades of green everywhere along the bed, hart's tongue ferns as fresh as green peas along the back, striped hostas, whose leaf patterns she thought looked 'like flames whizzing', arching out among more ferns below the retaining wall.

There are some true-blue hardy annuals for midsummer which she sowed straight into large flowerpots and left to flower where they stood: baby blue eyes (*Nemophila insignis*), small and shade-loving; *Echium vulgare* 'Blue Bedder', a thrilling garden form of the wild flower, viper's bugloss; and of course, love-in-a-mist to seed itself everywhere. She also sowed seed of the easy perennial, *Anchusa* 'Blue Angel', which bloomed all summer long with clusters of flowers 'like bits of an Italian sky', she said.

The whole idea had grown from a leap of the visual imagination – it was simple and bold, inventive and romantic. When the three arches and the 75cm (30in) pot were in position, the design was clear and painterly like an illustration in a picture book.

I first saw it when autumn was shading into winter. The big pot dominated the little garden. Over its edge the silver frosted

PLATE 7   *The untidy garden allows old roses to grow among long grasses on a steep bank of London clay above what was once a neat concrete yard.*

leaves of *Helichrysum plicatum* crinolined out wide and almost curtseyed, the stems curving downwards and then up again. Above them a smoke tree, *Cotinus coggygria* 'Atropurpureus' still held its purple leaves, with a depth of brown madder in them – or luminous copper when the sun shone through them. High above it rose a *Eucalyptus urnigera*, which I found easier to accept as a pot plant than as a street tree; it was still very young, a mere 2.5m (8ft) tall, slender and blue. You have to be prepared to cram things in like this, boldly, if you're short of space. Here were a tree, a shrub and a sub-shrub all sharing a 75cm (30in) pot, with white tulips round the edge waiting to appear in spring. The thing was like a dramatic foliage arrangement in an enormous vase: silver, smoky purple, glaucous blue. Luckily, the strict colour scheme did not apply to leaves, or the invaluable cotinus could not have been admitted.

Ann showed me a scale drawing of the garden. Plant names were pencilled in, she explained, so that she could rub them out when the plants died. Her resolution was tinged with fatalism. When I returned to the garden the next spring, she shrugged and said that the anemones, the lovely blue stars that should have been embroidering the earth, had simply not shown up. She had had to put a net right over the north-facing border to keep off the neighbours' cats. She had had to clip back their ivy because it was a favoured overwintering spot for snails. Those same neighbours had felled a tall willow that used to give shade and a sense of height and privacy on the northern boundary. On the opposite side a neighbour's japonica had boldly flung out an intruding branch covered in sealing-wax red blossom towards the soft blue clematis 'Frances Rivis', now reaching the top of its arch and covered in dangling flowers, each with four pointed sepals round a centre of white stamens. But the

PLATE 8   *Flagstones at sunrise on a formal rose terrace where informal carpeters spread between cracks and the severity of the original layout is redeemed.*

unplanned effect was pretty, and she had not the heart to cut back the japonica.

She pointed to a spike of the American bulb *Camassia cusickii*. Its starry flowers were distinctly lavender, yet the one she had seen at Kew (where she went at all seasons to search out her plants) had been blue. 'I suppose I shall have to give in on lavender,' she said.

But in the same corner as the disappointing camassia grew something which gave her that flooding pleasure which can instantly compensate a gardener for all manner of disappointments. It was an exochorda (*Exochorda* x *macrantha* 'The Bride'), a plant with associations that went back through her life. Her mother had grown it; there had been one at her school, a weeping, free-standing specimen on a lawn. Though there was no proper place for it in this backyard, she was determined not to be without it. She would grow it as a wall shrub, persuading its branches to weep along the wall. And here it was, still very small, but obedient to what she required of it and flowering all over. It was like a cross between a deutzia and a philadelphus; the flowers were single and came in clusters of eight, but what she particularly asked me to notice was that its flowers opened at the tip of the raceme first, while further back along the spray they remained in bud, small globes of white, like pearls. The open flowers, she said (for she had been drawing them) were rather like wild roses in form. And indeed, exochorda is a member of the rose family, the *Rosaceae*. The flowers have five petals, the stamens are gold, the leaves a fresh pale green.

She looked at all her flowers very closely like this, not only painting them but embroidering them on cloth. Along the chinks of the brick paving the little garlic bulb *Ipheion uniflorum* 'Caeruleum' was spreading, its flowers a washed-out blue so pale as to be almost grey; but what she liked, and pointed out to me, was the thin stripe of deeper colour down the middle of each petal at the back.

The next day I saw an exochorda in the packing shed of a

nursery I was visiting, weeping in its plastic pot. Impulsively I bought it. It will remind me, not of Ann's mother whom I did not know, but of Ann. That is the sentimental strand that runs through gardening, attaching one gardener to another.

The second small garden is in Shepherd's Bush. When Serafina bought it it was a dark, despondent square, more derelict than the original pink and perky Richmond garden 5.2 x 5.5m (17 x 18ft), with the usual corner missing where the kitchen jutted out. It was entirely overshadowed by a vast sycamore growing next door, and sycamore seedlings grew strongly among dandelions in the forsaken borders. Its floor was a cracked concrete screed and the fencing was woven panels. It had relatively wide raised beds round three sides, but their retaining walls were amateurishly concreted and thickly bulging. Someone had once planted some variegated ivy in the border; the cream and green leaves of the familiar *Hedera canariensis* 'Aurea Maculata' were dangling on a large section of the fence. This was the garden's only surviving plant.

Serafina negotiated, and paid for, the felling of the sycamore. After that she could not afford to rebuild the clumsy retaining walls, replace the panelled fences or root up the concrete screed. But she could, and did, use camouflage. She painted the concrete retaining walls with white emulsion. She bought bags of pea gravel at a local garden centre and spread gravel all over the concrete screed so that you could not see it any more. The space was transformed. Not only is gravel attractive in itself, it is also sympathetic to plants. Sylvia Crowe, in her book *Garden Design* (Country Life, 1958), describes gravel as 'recessive'. It does not come forward to catch the eye; rather, it throws the plants that surround it into the foreground. Along one edge of the gravel, where it met a raised bed, Serafina arranged large smooth pebbles collected from a beach, grey, sand-coloured and striped. As for the woven fencing panels – they would not show when covered in roses.

She was still too young to regard climbing roses as a

burden. She wanted, and must have, five favourite climbers: the redoubtable white climber 'Mme Alfred Carrière', to climb all over her north fence; the crimson 'Guinée', so velvet dark that it is almost shaded black, for the south wall of the house; for the west, the sentimental, warm 'Gloire de Dijon', palest French mustard to match its name, said to have grown in every vicarage garden of Victorian England; and two pink climbers, 'Aloha' and 'Caroline Testout', to share with a wisteria the southern wall. And that was not enough: she must also have a bush of her favourite rose, 'Papa Meilland', growing in front of these two pink climbers, itself a heady, perfumed crimson. Thus began Serafina's bower – not with a colour scheme, nor with a preconceived plan, but with a resolve to fit in a maximum number of favourite flowers.

She improved the soil. She had a friend with a livery stable, and each spring she heaved bags of rotted horse dung and straw through her narrow hall passage and kitchen, and spread them on her garden. As the flowers grew she tended them, watered them, fed them with foliar feeds. Now she patrols the garden for its legions of snails and slugs, starting in January by watering the whole garden with 'Nobble' in the hope of killing their eggs. It turns out that one dose of 'Nobble' cannot do the trick: regularly repeated doses are needed to reduce the slug-and-snail count, but any that survive she hopes to drown in plastic beakers of Guinness, sunk into the soil. The activity is continuous. The concrete walls must be re-emulsioned every March. Each March the pea gravel must be topped up. She is a busy professional woman, but this is her relaxation.

She gardens vertically. She sees her little plot as tiers of shelves, a small walk-in larder stored with treats. She plants in terms of levels, high flowers to hide the fence, low flowers to spill over and hide the concrete wall, ground-level flowers in pots on the gravel and, most important of all, middle-range flowers to meet you at eye-level if you sit on a white chair at a white garden table in a patch of sunshine, a glass of wine in your hand. The loveliest of these middle-ranking flowers are the arching ones, leaning out towards you: Solomon's seal, 45cm (18in) tall with pendant white bells in May; bleeding heart, the same height and habit and season, with dangling heart-shaped lockets of rose (but the drop of blood that falls from them is white); *Lilium regale* and *Lilium henryi* which open their trumpets in summer; and a tall, fresh green fern arching in a shadowy corner.

I like to imagine these as occupying the upper circle of the garden, and the garden itself, not as a store cupboard, but as a theatre. In the stalls are the pots: potted herbs round the back door (chives, mint, parsley, bay); then a neat dome of fresh blue-green *Hebe* 'Pagei', with the bloom of chilled green grapes on its leaves. There are also pots of transient things to come and go: bulbs and half-hardy annuals such as tobacco plants and white *Begonia semperflorens*. The loveliest of these annuals is the old-fashioned cherry pie, sweet-scented heliotrope.

In the dress circle the front row plants fall about, encouraged to cascade over the white-painted retaining wall. Some are a fresh green (feverfew, *Alchemilla mollis*), some are golden (creeping jenny – *Lysimachia nummularia*), some are silver (lamb's ears – *Stachys lanata* – and helichrysum), and some are purple (*Ajuga reptans* 'Purple Glow', and *Heuchera* 'Palace Purple'). Among the beautiful arching danglers in the upper circle sit, or stand, some erect herbaceous plants: purple *Campanula glomerata*, dusky acanthus, pink Japanese anemones. But these, too, tend to lean slightly forward towards the light, though they are all selected to be tolerant of the shade that falls over the borders by midsummer. Climbing above, in the gallery, the roses wave about among jasmine, honeysuckle and ivy. A bushy evergreen ceanothus grows up so tall that it looks like a small tree, and through it twine a clematis and a passion flower.

Serafina loves prettiness – hanging baskets brimful of annuals

– but she also loves subtlety: an eerie little grass whose leaves
are almost black and whose seed-heads remind her of black-
currants (*Ophiopogon planiscapus*), or an iris whose flowers
she describes as 'beige' (*Iris foetidissima*, the standby for dry
shade, whose flowers are indeed beige, like a fading bruise,
but whose following seed-pods are scarlet). In speaking of her
plants, she is rather like an indulgent mother. But if something
persistently refuses to flower, she is realistic enough to scrap it.
An agapanthus in a pot was nothing but a bunch of strap-like
leaves. 'It will have to go,' she said grimly. And whenever she
thus gains an empty pot or a square of bare earth, she savours
the delicious question: what can I put there?

In the shaded border nearest to her window she grows
winter and spring flowers. I visited her one March, when the
window-box was tightly packed with intense pink hyacinths, a
vibrant colour to cheer the heart. You looked over them and
saw the camellia, the wonderful 'Donation', its pot raised up
on a step at the opposite corner of the yard, dominating the
whole space as usual with its smother of double pink flowers.
But it did not have the whole space to itself. It could have
carried the garden but it was not asked to – indeed, it was
not allowed to, so much else needed to be fitted in. You saw
the pink camellia through a bank of hellebores – *H. corsicus*
and *H. foetidus* carrying high their weatherproof bouquets of
apple-green cups – and then, nearer to the camellia, *Helleborus
orientalis* held its dusky flowers closer to the ground: old-rose
splashed with green. Lower still, pulmonaria sprinkled pink
and blue above its spotted leaves, and the woodland borage
Omphalodes verna lifted up its large forget-me-nots. Behind
the sharp green hellebores the fence was covered with a pale
variegated ivy, so that the whole 2m (6ft) stretch of raised
border was brimming with pink shading to violet blue, pale
lime-green shading to cream.

'Did you choose pink hyacinths for the window-box on
purpose to go with the camellia?' I asked.

'No, it was luck,' she said.

And it was luck, she said, that made the *Helleborus orientalis* at the camellia's feet pink too.

Beyond the pink camellia, a white one waited in the wings. It would take over just as the flowers of 'Donation' dropped. If I had returned in April, I might have found that the potted narcissi on a lower step were cowslip-coloured, the potted tulips scarlet; the pink and green colour scheme would have dissolved into the brightness of yellow, scarlet and white. I did return in June. The border had sobered to green and white.

'It's lovely!' I said.

'But you should see Tina's garden!' she replied.

Tina's garden, in Fulham, measures 4.5 x 7.5m (15 x 25ft), longer than Serafina's but not as wide. When she moved in two years ago it was all ready and waiting for her. The walls were brick, there were raised beds on all three sides with brick retaining walls, and there was a choice climbing rose already planted ('Aloha' again, the repeat-flowering modern pink beauty). Perhaps it was a present to the previous owner from someone who had vicarious ambitions for that backyard. Nothing else had been planted there.

The floor was spread with Astroturf, synthetic garden carpeting which is not really the colour of grass, but a soft and inoffensive green.

Tina is a professional gardener, busy planting and maintaining the roof gardens and patios of customers who want decorative gardens but prefer to pay someone else to do them. She looked at her own new garden and decided to keep everything: the raised beds, the carpeting and the climbing rose. She simply added a 1m (3ft) trellis round the top of all three walls.

She worked to emphatic principles. First, a town garden must be year-round. And this involved her second principle: it must be largely a foliage garden, with a preponderance of evergreens. Evergreen? Ever-silver, ever-gold, ever-plum, purple, variegated. She would of course use the shrubs which had proved their worth in other gardens she had designed. There would be *Viburnum tinus* 'Variegatum' – 'nice and slow,' she thought, 'which is good for London', and less prone to look grimy than the plain dark green; the evergreen jasmine (*J. revolutum*) with daffodil-yellow flowers; *Elaeagnus pungens* 'Aurea-variegata', – 'it never looks anything but cheerful,' she thought, 'even in deepest shade.' She sat down and worked out her scheme. She would have a golden tree in the far corner on the left (*Robinia pseudoacacia* 'Frisia') and a blue-grey tree (*Eucalyptus gunnii*) in the far corner on the right. The left-hand west-facing border leading up to the golden tree would be filled with infinite variations of the yellow theme: hollies and ivies, privet, bamboo, box, the viburnum and the elaeagnus, all in varieties splashed or touched with yellow and cream among the shades of green, catching the afternoon sun. The east-facing right-hand border leading back from the eucalyptus to the house would be silver, pink, blue and white. And between the two borders and the two trees, at the end of the garden, a little pond with a fitted butyl liner could be built with a brick edging, a water lily, a water violet, water iris, and some water hawthorn. Over it could dangle the heart-shaped leaves, pink-tipped, of *Actinidia kolomikta*, a slender, shelter-loving climber.

Her third town-gardening principle was that, however small the space, it must have an air of secrecy. She made her garden into an hour-glass shape, not by any expensive structural alterations, but simply by the placing of pots: ten pots of varying sizes from huge to small were clustered together on the right, answered by an arrangement of six pots on the left, for too exact a balance might spoil the secret. The huge pot looked like terracotta but was in fact fibreglass, and in it grew another little tree, the weeping pussy willow *Salix caprea* 'Kilmarnock', spreading its decorous umbrella over two flourishing evergreen shrubs: a strawberry tree, arbutus, with bright evergreen leaves and little frosted fruit, and a rhaphiolepis with thick, handsome, egg-shaped leaves and small white flowers; they all shared the same potting compost and there was no sign that they grudged each other's presence. In front of this ambitious crowd came another slightly smaller pot dominated by a silver *Artemesia arborescens*, and towering over it a shining shrub of silvery green: *Pittosporum tenuifolium* 'Silver Queen'. It was strange to meet my common old Australian friend in this smart new context.

When first I visited the garden it was early September.

'I'm afraid it's a bad time to suggest coming,' I said.

'Well as a matter of fact,' she answered, 'the garden is looking rather good!'

She would never say: 'Oh, you should have been here last week,' or 'What a pity you couldn't come next month!' Her garden lived up to her principles: it was always fit to be seen.

The September sun was shining. The garden shimmered on the far side of sliding plate-glass doors that had been added to the back of the nineteenth-century cottage. Looking through any house into a garden is a pleasure, for the picture is framed, but it is particularly lovely to look from a town ground floor into depths of leaves. Afternoon light glinted on variegated silver and green. You could hardly see the white iron seat raised on a brick step on the other side of the promontory of ten pots. The pittosporum's leaves were dense; the little willow wept over clustered shrubs, its branches softly framing them. It was not so much a bower as a magic grotto.

The smaller, left-hand promontory was strong and spiky; a cordyline exploded its firework above a fringe of variegated felicia in magic blue, echoed by *Phormium tenax* 'Yellow Wave' and by the graceful leaves of a tall flag iris rising from the pond. Over the pond itself fell deep purple shades: a dwarf maple (*Acer palmatum* 'Dissectum Atropurpureum') in plum overlaid with olive was grouped with a berberis (*Berberis thunbergii* 'Atropurpurea Rose Glow') of smoky purple with a pink tinge.

Variegation vexes and divides people. It is highly favoured

today, as it was by the Victorians, but there remains a school of thought which shudders at the very thought of it. It is, some say, a freak of nature, a genetic mutation stemming from a virus. Yet variegation on a single leaf is only the microcosm of the variation between one plant and its neighbour in a well-filled border. Careful gardeners love to plant silver beside plum, or ivory beside green. When nature makes the mistake of variegating a plain leaf, she does not put two discordant colours together, but plays with gentle harmonies. Close-up, the variegations on Tina's plants were subtle. The shining silver pittosporum was, on close inspection, only edged with silver; the middle of each leaf was glaucous green. The privet (*Ligustrum sinense* 'Variegatum') had very slender leaves of delicate jade, ivory edged. The *Elaeagnus pungens* 'Aurea-variegata' was splashed, not with gold, but with lemon yellow on a background of sage green. *Hebe* 'Bowles' Hybrid' had leaves of polished mahogany whose base was sombre olive green.

If you love leaves so much, flowers may come and go at will. Of course she has flowers everywhere. Round a discreet long mirror behind the pond she has trained a wreath of the climbing rose 'Mrs Herbert Stephens' whose full white flowers hang downwards to admire their own reflection. In front of the inherited 'Aloha' the exquisite 'Margaret Merril', a modern floribunda rose that looks like a hybrid tea, grows behind potted regale lilies. Nearby is 'Rosemary Rose', the bright raspberry pink floribunda with flat, many-petalled flowers. Clematis twine through shrubs: the pink 'Hagley Hybrid' is pulled over the rosy berberis when it flowers; *Clematis armandii* climbs up the gum tree in early spring; 'Mrs Cholmondeley' opens huge flowers of lavender blue in June; *C. montana* 'Tetra-rose' wreathes the big windows (it is 'less violent', she says, than the other montanas). Down the narrow passage at the side of the house an orderly profusion of irresistible climbers grows together: 'Mme Alfred Carrière', the purple vine (*Vitis vinifera* 'Purpurea'), the miraculous passion flower in purple and lettuce green with stamens like the instruments of the cross, and the starry climbing potato, *Solanum jasminoides* 'Album', whose tiny flowers are not the usual mauve, but white – 'really divine', she says. Of course she has camellias and hellebores in winter, potted bulbs in spring, petunias and geraniums and lilies in summer, and 'only about ten fuchsias!' she says.

The density of it all is hard to realise. If you put your hand down between the plants you find there is barely a handspan between one stem and the next. Then you touch earth; it is moist, soft, weedless. There is a rich mulch of compost several inches deep. She waters every day in summer when it is dry, and never fails to dead-head every morning. Three times a year she has what she calls 'a great big chomp', cutting, training, thinning and, of course, eliminating. 'I am ruthless', she says lightly. Her robinia is not allowed to grow too tall. She cuts it back to what she calls a 'stump' in spring. 'It does not seem to mind,' she says, and laughs.

Tina laughs where other gardeners sigh. The whole garden breathes confidence and pleasure. She rejoices in everything – in the frogs who have moved into the pond, in the blackbirds who descend on autumn fruits, in the crinkly prickles of the little hedgehog holly, *Ilex aquifolium* 'Ferox Argentea'. 'Isn't it extraordinary,' she said to me one afternoon 'that people do nothing with their gardens when they could have so much pleasure?'

Her own pleasure is combined with years of experience. 'You have to *know* your plants', she says. 'You have to know what they will do.'

And yet I came away with the feeling that all her plants would do just what she wanted.

I went back to my daughter's garden. How empty and unenterprising it looked, great stretches of bare and stony earth between plants – why, there were only two roses, two shrubs, two fuschias and one vine in the whole raised bed! I bought a *Teucrium fruticans*, silver and powder-blue, and crammed it into a tight spot between two fuchsias and two brick walls, and tried not to think of Cinderella's ugly sisters struggling with the glass slipper. It looked crippled; Tina would have made it flourish. Intent now on density of planting, I began to bring back this and that from the country: *Alchemilla mollis*, the striped grass 'gardener's garters', black hollyhocks to stand against the whitewashed walls.

Next spring I returned to Tina's garden and gasped. There had been a metamorphosis. The green plastic flooring had been ripped up. It had gone soggy at the edges, she said, under all the pots and overhanging plants. Instead, her husband had laid York paving everywhere (a windfall from a relative's garden) and had dismantled the pond and rebuilt it a little to the left. The robinia had gone – altogether too big by now – and been replaced by a well-behaved *Acer negundo* 'Flamingo' which, like the pond, had been moved along a few feet. A delicate ferny creeper with what she admitted was 'a slightly boring yellow pea-flower', *Caragana arborescens*, now showed more clearly than before. The cordyline had not survived the winter, but a new one would be bought. The *Artemesia arborescens* was probably a casualty, cut down almost to the ground because it was taking up too much room in an important pot. The dividing promontory of ten pots had been dismantled, first for the laying of the stones and then for the rapturous admiring of them, once laid. But the silvery pittosporum looked lovelier than ever, and in front of it a pot glowed with pale apricot tulips.

Tina's enthusiastic happiness was fanned by a special purchase: she had just bought two cypresses in pots, trimmed like formal bay trees into balls, and placed one at each end of the Victorian seat. If Serafina's garden was the auditorium of a theatre, Tina's was the stage. The curtain had just risen on the second act, where the scenery had all been rearranged, and the white seat between the elegant standards was pulled forward, waiting for actors to take their places and a witty dialogue to begin. What would the last act be? The scruffy backyard had gone; now the bower seemed ephemeral too (see Plate 6).

These three gardeners neatly demonstrated the two poles of the gardening world which I had first glimpsed in my Melbourne childhood: the planters and the planners. Ann was the planner, who devised an overall theme in her mind before she bought a single plant. Serafina was the plantswoman, who started with a single favourite rose and worked out from there. And Tina was the point of balance between the two, working out her pattern in terms of the plants with which to express it. This was the difference between them.

Much stronger and more obvious was the thing they had in common. They all loved their gardens with a devotion that made them acutely aware of the health or sickness of every plant in their care. Like physicians, they did their ward rounds every single day, with observant eyes and patient diagnoses. At night, before falling asleep, each mused over improvements that might be made tomorrow.

IX

Untidy Gardens

What would the world be once bereft
Of wet and of wildness? Let them be left,
O let them be left, wildness and wet,
Long live the weeds and the wilderness yet.

Gerard Manley Hopkins, 'Inversnaid'

Gardeners divide into two groups: those who put tidiness
first, and those who don't. This is not another way of stating
the planter/planner division. You might expect the planners to
be tidy, but they are not necessarily so; an illusion of carefree
abandon was Edna Walling's signature. Planters may, or may
not, be messy; old Uncle George's garden was obviously neat
though of course, being a plantsman, he did not put tidiness first.

Exclusively tidy gardeners plant their daffodils evenly spaced
in rows, and knot their leaves into tight, old-maidish buns as
soon as they have finished flowering. They think a row of
twisted knots looks more seemly than a thicket of daffodil leaves
sprawling this way and that. (The daffodils do not enjoy this
treatment.) They don't allow plants to loll. They tie each stem
of a delphinium to a straight bamboo stake. They prefer bare
earth to ground cover. At the back of the tidy gardener's mind
is a half-formulated fear of the encroaching jungle – a wave of
anarchic plant behaviour which threatens to destroy the garden
the minute severe rule is relaxed. Behind this fear lurks another:
the fear of death. The process of dying must not be allowed to
show; when petals fall in the tidy garden, not only must they

114

be swept up at once but the seed-head of the flower must be removed.

When I first began to garden, it barely occurred to me to sweep at all. Sweeping was for indoors. But as I became more experienced and more observant, tidiness crept upon me. I reach for the broom when I see spilt earth on the path. I know that untidy town gardens encourage snails: they hide among crackly dead leaves or under forgotten flowerpots. Leaves left lying on the lawn kill the grass. Yet I, and my close friends, still fall temperamentally into the untidy-gardeners category.

One of my friends had a particularly untidy garden – so untidy, in fact, that it could scarcely be called a garden at all, and indeed she did not garden in it; her husband used it for his cuttings. He had green fingers, and for him the joy of gardening was the joy of propagation; he was not concerned to make his small backyard into a garden picture. There was a discarded kitchen chair of moulded orange plastic in one corner and, in another, a *Magnolia stellata* planted in a rubbish bin. It looked strangely tall, given this 60cm (2ft) lift off the ground. The only other plants were, inevitably, sycamore and forsythia; two self-sown forsythias grew strongly between old crazy paving and the wall, and a flourishing sycamore seedling aspired to become a tree by the kitchen steps.

'You don't actually need two forsythias,' I mumbled. 'One day, when there's something else you'd like, you could dig the little one out.'

'Right,' she said at once, totally amenable, not in the least defensive.

Her husband had become ill and could enjoy his potting no more. She had decided to 'do' the garden and we stood together, surveying it. Tidying, in this case, was imperative. We stuffed discarded plastic flowerpots into rubbish bags; we swept and swept; it was deeply satisfying. With all my strength, I pulled out the sycamore. The next time I visited, the orange plastic chair had quietly disappeared. Soon my friend found herself buying plants on the spur of the moment, containerised plants, already in tempting bloom. The first was a ceanothus. She dumped it at the foot of the steps and presently declared that it was not doing well, it did not like its pot. But it was the old story: she had not yet learnt to try the earth in the pot with her finger each day and, if it was not moist, to water it. She found some outsize earthenware flowerpots in her basement and bought a bag of John Innes compost number 3. We replanted her purchases in extra compost and beautiful big pots, watering liberally all the way along; we arranged them in likely spots against the walls. The ceanothus picked up, so did the pyracantha, the *Hydrangea petiolaris*, the mahonia, the honeysuckle, and the weigela. She encouraged me to be boss, but I tried not to blight her enthusiasm and say that whatever looked pretty at the garden centre at this moment was not necessarily the best long-term choice for her garden. The instant temptation of well-grown container plants in full bloom seduced her, but she sensed my disapproval. She phoned me half-apologetically one day.

'I have bought a yellow rose,' she confessed. 'It was very cheap.'

It turned out to be 'Canary Bird', the glorious, disease-free shrub rose with ferny, blue-green leaves and a profusion of little single blossoms shaped like strawberry flowers in May, so many of them that they scent the air. It was perhaps too big for the space, but there was a little patch of earth between concrete and wall where it could be inserted, and in time it would be able to spread its roots beneath the crazy paving. If we moved the ceanothus to stand beside it, the yellow and the powder blue would look so good together you would think the effect was planned.

Now we pulled the magnolia forward from its corner and placed it right below the window beside the kitchen steps where, paradoxically, the rubbish bin shows less and the magnolia itself shows more: the bin is below eye-level and hidden by some railings, the lovely strap-like white petals of the magnolia are lifted almost within touch. *Magnolia stellata* turns out to be happily tolerant of root restriction, whether in a rubbish bin or an expensive tub.

'Where does the sun strike?' I asked initially. She had no idea, but now she watches for it, and knows its movements; she waters and feeds. She is training the white potato flower, *Solanum jasminoides* 'Album', in a wreath along her iron railings; she is rapidily turning her backyard into another of London's leafy bowers.

That is a story of untidiness redeemed. But there are other sorts of untidiness exemplified by my other gardening friends.

One of them simply does not feel the threat of approaching chaos. She is impervious to the territorial advances that plants make when unchecked, for her plants exist, not so much in her garden, as in her mind. She is in search of *temps perdu*, seeking to recapture the rose that grows on the walls of her memory ('Gloire de Dijon'), or the bachelor's-buttons and tall Scotch roses, clipped like thimbles, yellow and white, in her grandmother's garden, or the violet rose, 'Reine des Violettes', that flourished in the garden of a friend. Like me, she taught English literature, and is thus equipped with a set of garden quotations to recite. If she could, she would plant a catalpa tree and a lime tree in her square patch of ground. This is because of Yeats's lines in 'The New Faces':

> If you, that have grown old, were the first dead,
> Neither catalpa tree nor scented lime
> Should hear my living feet . . .

The magic of trees' names speaks to her.

She remembers plant names, and instinctively recognises the superior beauty of certain plants: her garden is full of them. I first saw the vigorous early-flowering *Clematis armandii* in full riot along her garden fence and festooning her neighbour's evergreen tree with handsome leathery leaves and a milky way of starry flowers in March. When it stopped flowering a passion flower took over, its sharply detailed flowers suddenly appearing through the clematis leaves. She is unaware of overplanting, believing that there must be room for everything she wants because there is room for them all inside her head. She does not allow for their ultimate growth; for her, in her mind's eye, they are already full-grown.

But close, dense planting is fatal unless you are a Tina, prepared to stage-manage the scene, grooming and training the plants to fill the available space, boosting their tight-packed roots with water and liquid fertiliser. Otherwise, overcrowding is warfare with one coarse victor crushing many tender vanquished; choice paeonies drown in a sea of macleaya. Very occasionally she will uproot something, probably not with a spade but with her fists. And this is not so much to make more room for its neighbours as because she has what she calls 'negative thoughts' about it. 'Have rooted out hated mahonia, honeysuckle – hundreds of things,' she writes to me.

But she understands, intuitively, that good gardeners love their gardens. 'Better a dinner of herbs where love is,' she quotes, 'than a stalled ox and hatred therewith.' She thinks that it is her own impulsiveness that prevents her from being a devoted gardener. 'Impulsive people cannot be good gardeners,' she says, 'because good gardeners are faithful and true.'

This is only half the story. She simply does not feel that strong pull – whatever it is – that makes people break their backs and fingernails in flowerbeds. She could be faithful and true, but she would rather knit.

My third friend feels that pull. She is the gardener of the 'Buff Beauty' rose hedge, and her sort of untidiness is the untidiness of the wild-flower gardener and the nature lover. She moved some years ago from a big wild garden full of old-fashioned roses to a trim little garden of concrete slabs stuck together with cement, narrow borders, a cool pink mop-headed hydrangea and – inevitably – the 'Queen Elizabeth' rose. Beyond

the crazy paving was a patch of waste ground which sloped
sharply upwards. Someone had planted a Cox's and a Bramley
apple there and had marked out a little strawberry bed in rough
grass. It appeared that though the strip of land did not belong
to her and she could not put a fence round it she could use it.
She was the perfect custodian for that land. It did not occur to
her to cut the grass. Bright green lawns with knife-sharp edges
had no charms for her. Long grasses were her love. She, too,
had her special scraps of poetry to reinforce her tastes. She
quoted A.E. Housman to me:

> In acres of the seeded grasses
> The changing burnish heaves . . .

'The changing burnish' is perhaps the colour of the grasses'
shimmering seed-heads lifting in the breeze. She simply cut
paths, with garden shears, through her drying grasses, and
made random beds in the stiff London clay where they grew.
There was no topsoil – the clay had been flung up from the
railway cutting where the tube trains rushed below. But together
we moved the towering 'Queen Elizabeth' from its dominant
garden throne to an improvised bed in the clay. We damaged
its roots terribly in digging it up and only had ordinary peat
and bonemeal to plant it in, but it refused to relinquish its
life. After a period of shock it settled regally and grew taller
than ever in its new setting until it was sovereign, not only of
the garden, but of the waste land as well. The pink hydrangea,
which we also moved, was not so strong. It died. We felt bad,
but had not specially wanted it to live.

Now the old roses have moved in. Each year more beds are
hacked out of the clay, one bed per rose. They are not at all
affronted by being seen in the company of rough grass; they
are large, strong shrubs with nothing neat about them except, in
close-up, the exquisite arrangement of their petals. They mount
the bank in ranks one behind the other and because the ground

is sloping, you can see them all at once, the back ones peeping over the front ones' heads (see Plate 7).

There is the gallica, 'Charles de Mills', with infinitely crinkled and tight-packed petals of parma violet held in a shallow cup; there is the Bourbon rose, 'Boule de Neige', with incurved white petals making perfect big soft snowballs; then 'Stanwell Perpetual', ever-changing, ever-blooming, always neat, its small pink flowers fading to white, its pale buds opening to reveal creased depths of shell pink. And then there is the moss rose 'Mme Louis Lévêque', with huge pale pink cabbage flowers (for cabbages are neat in their way, too); and my aunt Bunny's old Alba, 'Céleste', pointed in the bud, opening to semi-double pink flowers lying flat among soft, grey-green leaves; and then 'Ferdinand Pichard', a hybrid perpetual with a pattern of delicate stripes on its petals – brushstrokes of rose on a base of white – giving the effect of milk streaked with raspberry juice. On what remains of a fence marking the boundary between garden proper and waste land, two specially favoured, strong-growing and lavish old roses make an arch. One is the many-petalled, intoxicating Bourbon, 'Mme Ernst Calvat', as heady as its famous parent, 'Mme Isaac Pereire' but a lighter, sweeter pink; and the other is 'Mme Hardy', the neat white rose with the green button eye in the middle, to many rose fanciers the favourite rose of all.

All these roses are scented. It doesn't matter very much in what order they come, they are like friends who mix well together, because they all belong to the cool pink/white/purple colour scheme with not a trace of orange or flame-colour or gold. Old roses fling their growths out sideways, arching, sprawling, and so, like well-trained climbers with horizontally tied canes, they break into flower all the way along their branches. Floribundas, on the other hand, have strong verticals, and reserve their flowers for the top. 'Queen Elizabeth' presents a veritable hedge of dark green foliage, fringed at the very top with pink. She is an unmistakable alien among the old roses. Though the pinkest of pinks, she has nothing to say to purple.

Her pinkness is unrelenting, there is no shading in it – it is the same all the way through on every petal at every stage of its growth. The arrangement of the petals is simple: no fluting, ruching or quartering is to be seen, therefore far fewer petals are needed to complete the picture. Fortunately she now towers so high that her flowers are seen, not against the old roses, but against the sky. She is a phenomenon; she will still be flowering when the old roses are resting. She has earned her position and will not be moved again.

Below her, a few more modern hybrids are gaining admittance. There is 'Cardinal Hume', one of David Austin's inspired English roses; it is as deep purple as the old gallica 'Cardinal de Richelieu' but, having part floribunda parentage, is repeat flowering. There are two new ground-cover roses, 'Grouse' (pale pink) and 'Partridge' (white), small and single like wild roses and ready to compete with the grass when the bluebells and buttercups are over. There is also a carpeting rugosa, 'Max Graf' – 'happy to racket along the ground,' she says. Most noticeable of all, there is the famous little carpeting rose 'The Fairy', filling a square metre with its tiny, bright pink rosettes among small, bright green leaves. It continues to flower when most of the others have faded, and is so well behaved that it is almost too good to be true; there is a faint suspicion that it may turn out to be artificial.

Not so with the unruly imperialist that carpets, not the ground, but the apple tree: *Rosa filipes* 'Kiftsgate' is flinging out its wild canes to conquer all the apple tree's branches, then suddenly, in July, scattering the largesse of its flowers – huge bouquets of little white blossoms – everywhere among the leaves.

Elsewhere in the garden things are on the move. My friend could not afford to scrap the crazy paving and replace it with big slabs, so she got a hammer and knocked a few holes through the concrete and cement. In the holes she planted thyme, thrift and *Phlox maculata*. She scattered Welsh-poppy seeds along the cracks, and by summer their frail yellow poppy flowers neutralised the bleak severity of the crazy paving. She put pots everywhere – apparently placing them at random, for any formality or pairing would have spoiled the carefree spirit of the garden. Now there are large ones, fat-bellied ones, ordinary ones and a tall chimney pot, and they hold a random mixture of plants: agapanthus, fuchsia, *Geranium phaeum*, *G. pratense* 'Johnson's Blue', nemesia, nicotiana. Other plants have begun to arrive, unbidden, straying from the little borders. Now there are clumps of *Alchemilla mollis*, harebells (*Campanula rotundifolia*), and clover. She welcomes them all; she only weeds out enchanter's nightshade, grass and plantains from her cracks.

How does one tell a wild flower from a weed? If you are an exclusively tidy gardener, no interloper is acceptable, so there is no problem. The garden is yours, not nature's, and you only allow in it what you have planted yourself. So you know that you cannot allow daisies in the lawn because you did not put them there. The minute they appear, you dose them with selective weedkiller and as they die you feel in control again. In my early gardening days, I was pleased when I managed to dig up a white bulb at the base of those unlicensed bluebells which were obliterating the straight lines of my tulip plantings. Now I know that groups of tulips rising among other flowers look better than tulips in thin lines, and I am allowing myself to love the encroaching bluebells all over again, because the gardeners I admire allow them in their gardens. They can grow here, but not there. They can grow so much, but no further. It is less easy to be an untidy gardener than a tidy one, because you have to judge each case on its merits, there is no rule of thumb. And in each case the plaintiff is the self-seeded flower.

A foxglove puts itself in the front of a carefully graded border. Forget-me-nots crowd in beside primroses, columbines and astrantia take over where lilies are meant to be alone, borage and alliums muddle up the pattern of the herb garden.

Should they be allowed to get away with it? Not if you want your own work in the garden to stand out plain for all to see. But if, instead, you want your garden to look as if it is an inevitable happening, something that simply evolved, then you will allow a shrewdly judged number of self-seeded plants to stay. They will be your allies in the creation of an illusion, and the ones that have put themselves in eccentric places will supply the most telling touches of all.

It is fun to tidy up a very untidy garden, but it is sheer joy to untidy a tidy one. I now know a beautiful big town garden which changed hands eleven years ago. It is on a steeply sloping site, but beside the house is a flat terrace, backed by tall clipped hedges of beech and pyracantha. The terrace is rectangular and paved in York stone. It has borders round two sides and there are two large rectangular rose beds set in the middle. When the new owners arrived these beds were each planted with three straight lines of roses, mirror images of each other: one line of red, one of white, and one of pink. The soil underneath the roses was bare. Here was the conventional formal rose garden for floribunda roses.

The new owner is a kindly gardener, reluctant to demolish plants. She liked the white 'Iceberg' roses and tolerated the anonymous pinks and reds, though when, in the course of time, the pink ones died, she did not replace them. She was busy underplanting the whole area with an apparently casual mixture of low-growing things, things with softly beautiful foliage, silver or blue-grey: lamb's ears (*Stachys lanata*) and rue (*Ruta graveolens* 'Jackman's Blue'); things that would flower in winter and spring: hellebores and pulmonarias and primulas; things for early summer: dicentras and London pride. 'Have you ever looked at the flower of London pride?' she asked, 'in close-up?' She pointed to the perfect centimetre of petalled precision, marked like an asterisk. Spectacle gave way to detail in those rose beds, and order to abundance, and the gawky stems of the old floribundas

disappeared from view, along with the straight stone edges
of the beds.

Meanwhile the cracks between the York slabs became
cracks in the neatness of the garden. Now self-seeding is
everywhere. *Alchemilla mollis* of course has colonised one
path, and *Campanula portenschlagiana* another. The little
yellow *Sisyrinchium brachypus* is spreading; the adorable white
daisy, *Erigeron mucronatus*, which shades, as summer advances,
into pink, makes a frilly trimming all along the steps that lead
up to the house, and spreads to mix with a bright pink silver-
leaved lychnis in the sun. The lychnis in turn mixes with rock
roses, *Helianthemum nummularium*, 'Wisley Pink', growing at
the feet of two great cistuses (*Cistus x aguilari* 'Maculatus'),
taken from cuttings and now warmly established against the
house walls. Given time, it seems, everything will stray from
the borders and colonise the paving (see Plate 8).

'Things *like* being in paving,' this devoted and tireless
gardener says. 'It's not too wet, not too dry. If they know
what they want,' she adds, 'good luck to them.'

Her tolerance extends to an errant broom, all tawny red
and yellow, which has sprung up in the corner of one rose
bed. She smiles, half-admiring, half-deprecating its cheekiness,
and leaves it be. Two hollyhocks have joined the paving party.
They don't look in the least cramped as they emerge from their
cracks and spread their great leaves over the stone, preparing
to soar upwards. They happen to have placed themselves symmetrically, like paired columns at the far end of the central
path. Did it simply happen, or are they two carefully selected
seedlings from a whole batch of less well-placed hollyhocks?
And where are the seedling grasses, the dandelions? A hand
has been at work, discreetly restraining nature while encour-
aging her.

The aim, of course, for all untidy gardeners, is the Paradise
garden – the garden of abundant fruitfulness, a place to be
happy in. But Adam and Eve were at work in their garden

before the Fall. Milton's Eve, in particular, was a tireless toiler behind the scenes. She warns Adam:

> What we by day
> Lop overgrown, or prune, or prop, or bind,
> One night or two with wanton growth derides
> Tending to wild . . .

and she suggests to him that he should

> Direct
> The clasping ivy where to climb, while I
> In yonder spring of roses intermixed
> With myrtle, find what to redress till noon.

Pruning, propping, binding, training – all is necessary if Paradise is to be regained. Gardening *is* tidying. But good gardening directs attention, not to the tidiness, but to the garden.

X

Patterned Gardens

Grove nods at grove, each Alley has a brother
And half the platform just reflects the other . . .

Alexander Pope, Epistle IV: 'Of the Use of Riches'

Across the river Thames at Lambeth Bridge, in the churchyard of St Mary-at-Lambeth, there is a knot garden. It is a square with a circle fitting exactly inside it. The circle is subdivided in its turn by four arcs or semicircles which combine to make regular petal shapes of the sort one learnt to draw in childhood, holding a pencil screwed into a compass, when suddenly geometry lessons shaded into art. In the sixteenth and seventeenth centuries, and again today, gardening shades into geometry, and the pencil lines become low hedges of moss-green box dissected, at intervals, by ice-green santolina, all clipped into such neatness that the pattern is clear. Halfway between the circumference and the centre of the Lambeth garden there is the suggestion of a second square, broken on four sides where the pattern of the four petals intersects, and in the middle, where the compass point would have rested if this were a diagram and not a garden, there is a neat clipped variegated holly.

Shrub roses, herbs and simple hardy annuals grow together in the well-defined spaces between the low hedges. So firm is the framework that the plants can do what they like within it: tall bushes of the old apothecary's rose (*Rosa gallica* 'Officinalis')

126

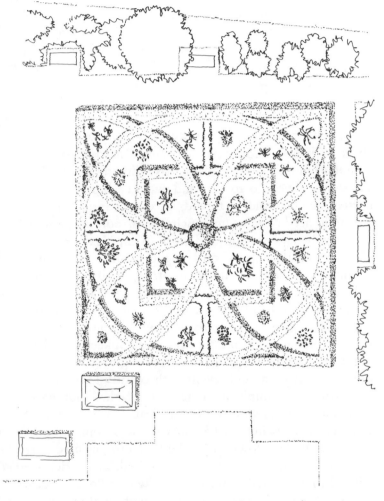

The knot garden at the Museum of Garden
History, Lambeth. A four-petalled flower and
a circle combine to fit inside a square, all
defined by clipped santolina and box.

can burst into bright pink in one compartment, and in another low orange marigolds can flower without seeming to clash with the neighbouring pink; the discipline of pattern keeps the plants in order. Pattern-making such as this has the absolute rightness of a problem solved. It is a garden dedicated to the memory of the John Tradescants, two great gardeners whose family tomb stands nearby: 'A world of wonders in one closet shut . . .', as the epitaph carved on the top of the tomb explains. No flowers bloom here that were not blooming in the seventeenth century, when the knot garden was the fashion of the day.

It is back in fashion now, and newly married couples can twine their initials into a knot of box, clipping the little hedges so that they appear to go over and under each other where they intersect like embroidery threads. It can fit into a small town garden; it needn't take up much room, nor much time, for short, low hedges are not hard work to clip. It can be designed on paper and then transferred to the ground with lines, pegs or templates. There is a move afoot, especially in smart front gardens, to do away with grass and flowers and concentrate on box and gravel and Victorian edging tiles. Perhaps these are gardens belonging to non-gardeners who employ professionals to lay out their gardens and specify ease of upkeep, but the move is back towards the patterned parterres of gravel and box which evolved in sixteenth- and seventeenth-century France.

A parterre is simply an extension of the knot garden – larger and more obviously symmetrical. On a summer day I stood at a window in the Château Vaux-le-Vicomte in northern France and looked down on to the Le-Nôtre-inspired parterre. You could see the idea from above; indeed, the garden seemed designed to be looked at thus, from the first-floor windows. It was spread out like a Persian carpet, a pattern of rectangles and lozenges and squares holding smaller patterns within them. The colours were gravel colours, together with the pink of brick dust and grey limestone chips, curving in arabesques among spiralling twirls of box. There were obelisks of yew and narrow bands of grass along straight paths; marble busts on pedestals marked the edges of the parterre and ornamental fountains marked the axial views.

Suddenly I saw why the aristocrats of pre-revolutionary France were proud to have gardens like this. It was clearly not with any thoughts of saving time on upkeep, but because such gardens are the same winter and summer; they are impervious to the seasons, and represent the triumph of man over time, the defeat of nature, an illusion of power and permanence in the face of change. They are a far cry from the pretty knot garden at Lambeth which is full of flowers in summer, changing to sobriety in winter, a happy mixture of freedom and control.

In England, parterres are filled with bedding plants, not gravel. They come in blocks of colour – one or two colours per bed, and ideally the bedding plants are the same height as the clipped hedges that define them. But what if you take away the hedges? You are left with carpet-bedding, which is still pattern-making but tends to be despised. Parterres are in fashion, carpet-bedding is out.

Yet it seems narrow-minded and doctrinaire to rule out carpet-bedding. Outside my window in a public square are four curved beds round a statue. They are brimful of scarlet geraniums and purple verbena with an edging of white petunias and a crescent of deep pink petunias with starfish stripes of white. Children are running round the beds, their mother is sitting on a seat in the shade facing them. On the far side, cars are streaming past, but the bright flowerbeds help us to ignore the traffic, enjoy the sun, and feel that life is gay. I notice that there are also some lemon-yellow African marigolds used as dot-plants in the scheme.

The other two beds, which complete the circle, are planted with floribunda roses. Their first flowering is over; they are quiescent, a dull green with expanses of bare hoed soil between them. The planting is clearly an economy move: last year the whole circle of four beds was devoted to brilliant bedding. I find that I miss it now half of it is gone.

The curious thing is that bedding schemes can get away with clashes, just as knot gardens (and kelim rugs) can. Purple and scarlet and yellow can mix amiably together provided there is enough of each, and that neutralising colours are used too. When the young plants first start to reveal their petals we may cringe. 'Oh no!' we cry. But as they grow and the total pattern develops, the eye accepts them and blends them together into a single vibrant blur.

Municipal bedding is expensive in time. A team of five men spent the best part of a day lying out the little plants with marvellous accuracy according to a master plan. No doubt another team of men had spent weeks raising them under glass. In the autumn the square's regular gardener will dig them all up, throw them away, fork over the beds, and the team will move in again to plant a pattern of hyacinths, tulips and polyanthus for next spring. At least, I hope they come.

I know a professional gardener who works in a municipal garden by day and tends his own garden in the evenings and at weekends. He has erected greenhouses in his back garden and there he raises scores of half-hardy plants. When the danger of frost is past, he moves them out and creates his carpet-bedding scheme. He lives in a little semi-detached house whose front door is diagonally opposite its gate. The path takes a reversed 'S' curve between gate and door, with six standard roses along one side as regular as an avenue of pleached limes. Along the fence are planted out another regular row of standard fuchsias interspersed with abutilons whose pale maple-shaped leaves are freckled in cream. The coloured carpet is spread richly below these miniature avenues of vertical stems. There is an edging of lobelia on one side, feverfew and busy lizzie on the other. Tall specimens of impatiens are slotted in between the standard roses with French marigolds at their feet. In a sloping bed opposite, scarlet and shocking-pink petunias are mixed together, regularly interspersed with the taller, purple-leafed fuchsia 'Thalia' and the shorter lilac-blue ageratum. The discord is dazzling, but disciplined to the last leaf. Individual plants are of no importance here. They are not meant to be examined close-up, but to have carrying power. Their job is to be the same as their neighbours, like Ziegfeld girls all kicking their legs to exactly the same height. The aim – achieved with absolute confidence and professional skill – is to create a living, three-dimensional pattern of colour, wall-to-wall.

Gardeners are subject to these contrary pulls: the pull towards pattern, and the tug towards the wild. The Chelsea Flower Show reflects these contrary leanings. It has always catered for carpet-bedding fanciers with its improbable and spectacular pyramids of half-hardy annuals mounted by the great seed houses and, more recently, by the boroughs' parks departments. But today it presents, in sharp contrast to each other, the fashion for formality and the longing for the natural. Weeds and wild flowers have moved into the marquee. Exhibitors now place artfully selected weeds on the edge of paths, and John Chambers' stand of fresh and gentle wild flowers draws us away from displays of gaudy artificiality across the aisle, to pretend for a moment that we are standing in a summer field. At the same time, all up and down Eastern Avenue the clipped topiary, the spirals and obelisks of box and bay, can be bought, at a price, in Versailles tubs. A maze – the apotheosis of the knot garden – is constructed out of yew in green and gold, to combine significant symbols and monograms for the ingenious to discover. Curiously enough, the very people who love the wild flowers also love clipped box and yew. I know, because I find that I am one of them.

In fabrics, I like floral chintz but I also like checks and stripes. In gardening, I love overflowing exuberance but also pretty trellis, basket-weave brick paving, straight lines and symmetry. I visit other people's gardens, happy to discover disordered abundance but inspired when, very occasionally, I come upon real pattern-making. I am thinking of two expertly patterned gardens: one of straight lines and squares, the other of circles.

The straight garden (measuring 13 x 5m) is beside an end-of-terrace house whose front door itself is at the side, so the garden serves both as a front garden and as a back garden for sitting in. It used to be unkempt and dark, with a chestnut tree overshadowing thick undergrowth. Now it is light: half in sun, half in shadow, patterned, paved and trellised. The chestnut tree has gone.

Because it was surrounded on three sides by high brick walls, the place reminded its designer (James Sutton) of Parisian courtyards where *treillage* alone is used to convert a light-well into a garden. Trellis is expensive; the designer and his son (whose garden it is) made their own, using lathes of beech and pine taken from piles of discarded pallets. The only cost was in some cans of creosote. They made simple squared trellis for the house walls, between and below the windows, and for the high wall opposite. But then they made six beautiful and ambitious arched panels – three to go across the end of the garden and three more set into the facing wall, the middle one exactly opposite the front door. The series of arched panels had the repetitive satisfaction of a colonnade and the elegance of the round-topped windows found on the ground floors of Regency terraced houses. Porthole-like circles of trellis were fixed in the spaces between the arches to complete the design at the top. At the bottom, two large and important square oak tubs, each planted with a sphere of clipped box, were made to stand in front of the trellising, opposite the front door.

Now, at the end of the garden in front of the central arch, a little fountain plays into a semicircular pool. The pool is faced with leaded plates rather like fish scales, and has a wide silver-grey rim which might be stone but is in fact oak, inviting you to sit down and dabble your fingers in the water.

There are four flower borders, two sunny ones on either side

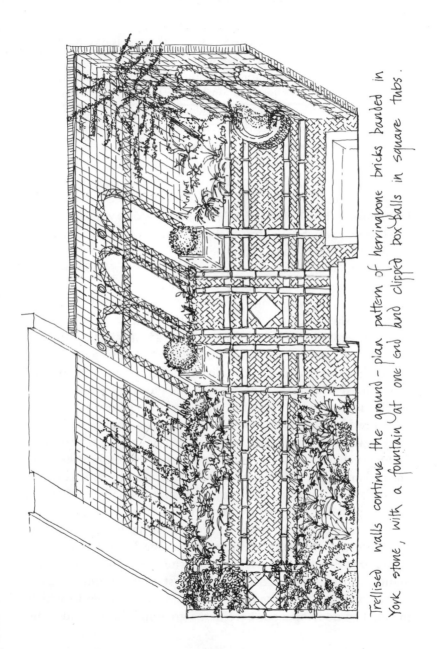

Trellised walls continue the ground-plan pattern of herringbone bricks banded in York stone, with a fountain at one end and clipped box-balls in square tubs.

of the front door running along beneath the windows, and two correspondingly shady ones opposite. All the rest is paving, brick and stone, but more brick than stone, as stone is so expensive. The bricks are second-hand London stock bricks of mellow clay-colour. They are banded with four lines of grey stone in single flagstone width running down the length of the garden, and six lines across the width; where they intersect they make an unfussy checked pattern, and the central check is marked with a large square paving stone set crossways, a diamond inside a square. The whole composition is so exactly adapted to the measurements of the site that it might always have been here. The finishing touch is a young hornbeam hedge with a central gap through which you approach what has become a courtyard of perfectly judged formality (see Plate 5).

The garden of circles is bigger: 7.5 x 13.5m (25 x 44ft), typical of suburban back gardens everywhere. When its owners moved in, thirty years ago, they found (as we had done) an Anderson shelter in the middle of what used to be the lawn. But they exploited theirs, while we cursed ours. They started by carrying armfuls of concrete through the house to a skip in the road; a great mound of rubble and earth remained. Patiently they moved it all to the bottom of the garden, spread it out, levelled it and built a retaining wall, and thus gained one of the most precious assets any garden can have: a change in levels. They paved the higher level (there would have been no point in sowing such a narrow strip with grass), built a compost heap at one end and a garden shed at the other, each to be concealed by thick planting in front. It became a lush and shady place with a recumbent fatshedera spreading over stones. The rest of the garden was nice, but ordinary: a rectangular lawn with stepping stones down one side running along a side border, a morello cherry tree planted against the opposite wall, and a towering mature ash tree in a corner. The most inviting thing was a terrace outside the house on a level with the lawn on to which the kitchen door opened; here herbs grew in a barrel and ferns grew in fine old chimneypots rescued from the roof. It became an outdoor dining room with a slate-topped table underneath a pergola.

Seven years ago the ash blew down in a high wind, bringing the wall down with it and wrecking the morello cherry tree. The garden looked a ruin, and depression hung in the air. Then the insurance paid for a new wall and new hopes rose; depression gave way to excitement as the owner, an exhibition designer (Robin Wade), got out his drawing board and redesigned his garden.

He was bored with the straight path of stepping stones beside the straight border. He wanted to escape from the rectangular lawn into the illusion of a circular one. He didn't mind if the circle was incomplete; in fact, he preferred the idea of a large circle of grass which had lost a stretch of its circumference to a smaller, completely circular lawn. The important thing, as he delighted to explain, was to mark the centre of the circle firmly – that crucial point where the compass rests. He marked it with a tree – a new morello cherry, planted as a freestanding specimen towards one side of the old lawn. The new lawn was measured from the cherry tree, sweeping freely round it until it ran into the boundary wall on one side. It was a brilliant trompe l'oeil: though the wall seemed to obscure your view of the completed circle, your inward eye supplied it. There was no conventional flower border at the foot of this wall – that would reinstate the very rectangle from which the garden was escaping.

The idea of the circle was carried into happy details on the side where the sweep was interrupted: a short section from a lesser circle, like an inner ripple from a stone thrown into water, was marked out on the grass in brick; a blacksmith was instructed to make curved metal baskets like window-boxes – another ripple, to be fixed waist-high on the wall. The pergola over the dining terrace was adapted to fan out as if to describe another section of the circle.

The straight path was gone. The circular edge of the new

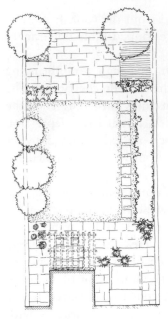

Here is a typical
back-garden: lawn in
the middle, path down one
side and paving at each end.

lawn was neatly edged with bricks for clarity of definition.
The old flower border remained, now following the new
edge of the lawn, and a great sweep of oak trellis, erected
in the border, lifted the idea of the circle from lying flat on
the ground up into the air. This curved trellis prevented the
eye from dwelling on the straight boundary wall behind the
border; it was not intricately latticed all the way round, for
that would have hidden the flowers behind it at the point
where it curved forwards; it was strictly see-through at this
point, with wide-apart lathes, and each panel was joined with
an elegantly carved finial at the top. Further along, it became
a closely trellised little arbour round a cast-iron seat in the
familiar Victorian fern pattern which is usually painted white.
But Robin Wade repainted his seat a sympathetic, unobtrusive
green.

A pattern like this could only evolve with careful calculation
on the drawing board first. Now that it is done, it is not only

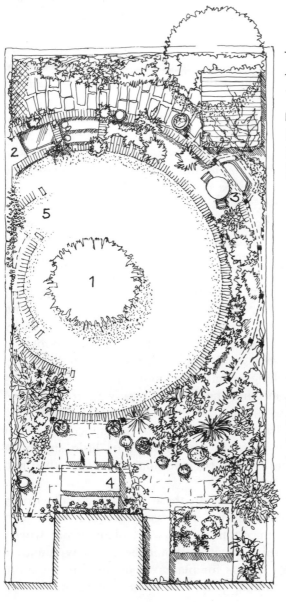

The same garden
transformed.
The centre of the
uncompleted circle
is firmly marked
by the cherry
tree.

1 morello cherry
2 pond
3 seat
4 slate table
5 arc of bricks

far more interesting than the old rectangle, but also clearly more interesting than a completed circle would have been. It stretches space, adds mystery to the certainties of pattern, and the whole garden has expanded into a place that invites you to explore. Round the other side of the wall, you feel, there is more to be seen. The wall itself is hidden under a curtain of the 'Kiftsgate' rose.

But the designer is still not satisfied. The stone terrace outside the kitchen door remains part of the earlier plan, uncompromisingly straight. He would like to lay lines of bricks radiating across the stone, pointing the eye back towards the cherry tree. He will not be content until his whole garden is in harmony with its central theme.

And even then he will not be content. He has made a small deep pool beside the central steps which now lead up to the higher level at the bottom of the garden. It is cool, 1m (3ft) deep, built of brick and tanked with mastic; the bricks at the front have been sliced thin so that the water comes as near to the edge as possible. Small goldfish swim in it and frogs croak; above it, a stone gargoyle, sold off years ago by York Minster, dribbles from its weird mouth. The pool is a delight, but it is very small. He has a vision of doubling his water garden, making a matching pool on the other side of the steps and connecting the two by a very narrow channel cut at the back of one of the steps. You would simply step over shallow water as you passed to the upper level. But his wife says no: there is the question of little stumbling grandchildren. And there is the question of the flowerbed and flowers.

Neither pair of gardeners in these two patterned gardens claims to be plantsmen; in each case there has been great interest and some uncertainty over what plant to put where. In strongly designed gardens it should be this way round: a question of finding 'plants for places' as opposed to the more usual question of finding 'places for plants', the problem with which every hopeful gardener is familiar, returning home one day with an impulse buy.

The designer of the circle garden had, not surprisingly, a liking for shapely plants – plants with a good sense of design themselves. His garden is full of beautiful leaf shapes and beautiful textures. The polished leaves of *Magnolia grandiflora* grow against the corner of the house; fig leaves spread along the wall behind the dining table; on the pergola overhead is a canopy of grape vine and *Vitis coignetiae*, bright green vine leaves against richer, softer ones. Through spaces in the flagstones on the terrace strong acanthus spread their deep-cut glossy leaves beside the matt grey-green leaves of *Echinops ritro*: prickly, sombre spikes of hooded flowers rise against tall stems topped with powder-blue balls. Behind them stands a handsome white plaster-cast of a classical column (salvaged from the British Museum where Robin Wade designed the sculpture gallery). Beyond, the towering Scotch thistle, *Onopordon acanthium*, spreads out its stiff silver candelabra. At its feet a variegated form of the New Zealand flax, *Phormium tenax*, shoots stiffly outwards, and at its side the plume poppy, *Macleaya cordata*, soars upwards, as soft as the phormium is spiky (see Plate 2). There are many rushy leaves in the garden: tall, looping flag irises, graceful bamboos. An abundant *Clematis armandii* with its handsome, three-lobed evergreen leaves spreads right across the trellis behind the pond covered in its scented white flowers in early spring. There are hostas, and ferns everywhere: ferns growing casually against the wall, a magnificent royal fern (*Osmunda regalis*) rising beside the little pond, its seed-heads bronzy copper. On the upper level at the bottom of the garden three apple trees are espaliered against the wall as an extension of the patterning: 'Spartan', 'James Grieve' and 'Granny Smith'. The big round leaves of bergenia soften the edges. In summer, the dominant feeling of the garden is an encircling leafiness.

The dominant feeling of the other garden – the paved and trellised one – is of cool, elegant white. Its owners, new to gardening, went to Sissinghurst and returned inspired, not by the dusky violet-tinted border nor by the yellow, red and sunset cottage garden, but by the white one. Vita Sackville-West had written in an *Observer* article: 'I am trying to make a grey-and-white garden. This is an experiment which I ardently hope may be successful, though I doubt it.' In the event, the success of her experiment has spread through the land. Is it because white goes so beautifully with green, and with all leaf colours – silver, grey and gold as well? Is it because there are so many lovely white flowers that it makes choosing simple, and mixing easy? Or is it because the white version of a favourite flower always seems to spell extra refinement and make the original colour seem obvious and slightly vulgar? Long ago Eileen had told me that white lilac is more desirable than purple. My friends prefer *Magnolia stellata* to *Magnolia soulangiana* because it is pure white, unstreaked with rose. But when this happens I feel the stirrings of a revolt within me – the obstinate move back towards the mauve, the purple and the pink.

White flowers remain beautiful in a town garden. And here, in this courtyard, the trellises are waiting to be clothed in climbers – green leaves and white flowers – and are even in danger of being submerged, one day, in white roses. Already the never-fail climbing form of 'Iceberg' is growing in the sun, along with 'Mrs Herbert Stephens', 'Sander's White' and the prolific 'Wedding Day'. 'Mme Alfred Carrière' grows opposite, in the shade. In the four borders, white flowers for shade on one hand answer white flowers for sun on the other. There is no problem in filling the beds, for almost every lovely plant you can think of has a white version. If you like oriental poppies, you can have 'Perry's White' which, complete with trembling indigo stamens and splashes on its petals, is absurdly more showy than its scarlet counterparts. You can have white lavender (*Lavandula* Nana alba), white paeonies, white delphiniums, white agapanthus (*A.* 'Bressingham White', white potentilla, white irises, white pinks. They have planted most of these already. In the shade they have a white camellia (*C. alba plena*), a mock orange (*Philadelphus* 'Manteau d'Hermine'), Solomon's seal and *Smilacena racemosa*, St Bernard's lily (*Anthericum liliago major*), white foxgloves, lilies, hostas, Japanese anemones (*Anemone japonica* 'White Giant') and white primulas. The white form of bleeding heart (*Dicentra spectabilis alba*), originally planted in the sunny border, is moving to dangle its white Dutchman's breeches in the shade. The large-flowered clematis 'Marie Boisellot' is trained up one side of the front door, *Magnolia grandiflora* 'Exmouth' on the other, and a white wisteria is beginning to climb the corner. Pots of white geraniums are mixed with ferns to stand round the semicircular pool. In spring there are snowdrops, dwarf daffodils (*Narcissus triandrus albus*), the dwarf tulip *kaufmanniana* 'Chopin' and white parrot tulips. In winter there are *Prunus subhirtella* 'Autumnalis' and *Clematis armandii* because, apart from being the top winter plants of every wise town gardener, they happen to be white as well. At midsummer all the empty spaces in this still-new garden are filled with white tobacco flowers.

White flowers make their own pattern. And of course, as the workers know, they show up best at night. They are gently restorative after the dust of traffic, and they are often highly scented as an antidote to traffic fumes. White is not strident; it is an inward-looking colour. It helps to make this front garden seem like a back garden and the public place seem private.

Clearly, I would be cheating if I pretended that these two gardens, in their skilful patterning, belong in the same category as knot gardens and parterres and carpet bedding. Knots and parterres are decorative episodes, like embroidery on the fabric of a garden. But the total pattern of a garden is like the cut of a coat — tailoring rather than embroidery — and these two gardens are designers' work: full-scale integrated compositions that would not be despised by Gibberd or Jellicoe. Being able to measure up your garden plan on paper is only a means to an end. You have to be able to think in three dimensions; you need, like a sculptor, a sense of space, and of the relationship between different spaces. But if you get it right, it will be such a rare satisfaction that choosing plants to fill it can seem merely incidental.

Or so I thought, until at last I came to a garden where the plantsmanship was of such calibre that I had to adjust my scale of values. I found myself back at the beginning again, learning to garden.

XI

The Beautiful and Rare

I cannot see what flowers are at my feet,
Nor what soft incense hangs upon the boughs
But, in embalmed darkness, guess each sweet . . .

John Keats, 'Ode to a Nightingale'

At first I was only aware of flowers. They were all round
me, on both sides, as far as the eye could see. The colours
were lavender-blue and lilac-blue and violet, silver and lemon-
yellow and cream, apricot, tawny-red and wine-red and plum.
Or perhaps all the colours were there, but blended by such a
skilful hand that nothing clashed, every colour was a gentle foil
for its neighbour. Above all, there was green – a multitude of
greens, filling the borders, blocking out the walls, so that there
appeared to be no boundaries. In fact, the boundary walls were
only 5m (16ft) apart; I was back in a very long – 38m (125ft) –
and narrow garden; I was back in Grove Terrace. It had been
a case of the old gardeners' network.

'So you used to live in Grove Terrace. Did you know
Lucy Gent's garden?'

'No.'

'Oh, but it's wonderful. You must see it. I'll write to her.'

The kind intermediary fixed it up. I drove across North
London and parked, like a fugitive, in a side street. The present was half-obliterated by the past; I walked again down the
sloping pavement with the little front gardens on my left and
the municipal lawns on my right and the ghosts of my children

143

and my neighbours' children running ahead. And of course Lucy Gent's house turned out to have the aromatic front garden where the ground-cover rose 'Nozomi' and the cistus and lavender and *Aster latifolia* grew.

It was August; the leaves on the plane trees lacked lustre. And it was pouring with rain. She opened the front door and we went through to the back and looked out of the sash window at the garden. The rain was falling in relentless vertical lines and splashing on to flagstones. York paving stones change colour when they are wet; they look warm rather than cold, yellow-green (almost khaki) rather than grey, sleek and light-reflecting. And through the rain the flowers glowed.

But it was *Hydrangea villosa* that filled the view. There it was, as if transplanted from old Bunny's garden a few yards down the hill, even more beautiful here, a mature specimen spreading its low branches grandly across the paving and caught at the perfection of its flowering, when the small fertile flowers in the centre of its panicles are intense parma violet and the starry outer flowerets are blue touched with pink. It was 2m (6ft) tall and 4.5m (15ft) wide; it half blocked the view down the garden; there was a glimpse of golden-lily trumpets beyond. An audacious self-sown blue campanula had the inspired cheek to grow through it, giving the illusion that this was a garden that had simply happened. Above it were the improbable white stars of a large-flowered clematis. A second shrubby hydrangea grew between it and the house, *Hydrangea sargentiana*, with enormous drooping felted leaves, handsome but sober, prepared to act as a worthy partner to *H. villosa* without in any way upstaging its act, for *H. sargentiana* grows upwards while *H. villosa* spreads outwards; there was no danger that its flowers would be hidden.

On the paving in the angle between the two hydrangeas stood a shapely black empty garden pot, 45cm (18in) tall. 'Black' is not quite right; it was charcoal, or terracotta overlaid with ink; it had the tints within a bunch of purple grapes. Its plump sides were striated, and behind it the fronds of a bright green fern seemed to echo, in their parallel leaflets, the lines etched on the pot.

Opposite, across the flagstones, a low brick retaining wall surrounded an ancient yew, and on this low wall sat another pot, a pale disc of extreme simplicity, smooth as ivory. The paved space between the woodland hydrangeas on one side and the majestic yew tree on the other spread wide, with an almost austere grandeur and a sense of limitless space; you felt that if you lifted the hydrangea branches you would find the paving continued beneath them. The generosity of its sweep defied you to find this garden 'narrow' or to call the paving a 'path'; it only became a path as it led on round and beyond *Hydrangea villosa*'s sweeping branches.

We went out, under umbrellas. She was tall, I was short, so our umbrellas did not hit each other. Neither of us said a word against the weather, though we may have laughed a bit at the absurdity of it, as we slowly progressed down the garden.

I simply did not know what these flowers all round me were. I took refuge in asking all the time: 'What's that? What's that?' Such anxious questions can sap the pleasure from a richly planted garden where the mystery is part of the excitement, but we garden visitors feel obliged to ask them. Perhaps we think that only by putting a name to a flower can we get a hold on its beauty, or perhaps we think that we must discover the name so that one day we might grow the plant ourselves. Lucy was infinitely patient and cheerful in spelling out the Latin.

'What is this lovely lemon-yellow thing?'

'*Nepeta govaniana* – just a catmint, with yellow flowers.'

'What are these charming things in pots with pink and white flowers?'

'*Francoa ramosa* – half-hardy, much loved by Gertrude Jekyll.'

'What's that large-leafed thing with flowers like angelica?'

'*Aralia cachemirica* – Christopher Lloyd raves about it in his catalogue.'

We did not linger indefinitely over name-dictation, because the pull of the continuing garden path was too strong. There was the next 'thing', and the next, to marvel at. It was so densely planted that it seemed even longer than it was because we had to go so slowly; its length became its strength; we walked on through a series of spaces, first over paving, then across bricks, then grass, then along a narrow path of plum-coloured tiles, always between strange and lovely flowers, always with a sense of fluttering excitement at the hidden possibilities ahead. We came to another ink-dark vase, tall and graceful and filled with a purple heuchera (*H. micrantha* 'Palace Purple') which seemed to borrow its colour from the clay; it almost stopped us, like a punctuation mark. When we left it behind us, we saw another dark vase ahead – this time shorter, plumper, filled with shrubby honeysuckle (*Lonicera reflexa*). The garden was thus divided into chapters, like the other long and narrow terraced gardens I knew, but the story was so enthralling that you barely paused at the end of one chapter before starting the next, and when at last you reached the end you had to go back to the beginning again. The journey back was another story. Just as a country road looks quite different according to the direction in which you are travelling, so this garden looked quite different on the journey back towards the house. Besides, you could not notice everything on the journey out (see Plate 3).

'Come back again when it isn't raining,' she said.

I have been back in autumn, winter, spring and midsummer. I have now seen the garden shimmering in brilliant sunshine when the light shines through the leaves. ('That's *contre jour* effect, I think,' she said.) I have sat in it alone on a seat halfway down on a May morning when a blackbird was singing his liquid aria in a pear tree opposite, and beside me a dry-looking grey-green shrub, a summer-weather shrub, reminded me of the Australian seaside, as did the warm, resinous scents of the low-growing herbs at my feet. (I later learnt that the shrub is called *Dorycnium hirsutum*, a member of the pea family.)

I have also seen the garden full of people on an Open Day. They, like me, had notebooks out. They asked about an eye-catching herbaceous plant on the edge of the path whose starry flowers opened from pink calyxes.

'*Gillenia trifoliata*,' said Lucy, continuing her unpatronising dictation of proper names.

'What's *that* thing?' they were saying. 'What's *that?*' In particular, they asked the name of the beautiful little specimen tree with three stems that stood at the bottom of the garden.

'*Cercidiphyllum japonicum*,' she said.

How would they remember if they did not write it down? Sometimes she wrote it down for them.

But I now know what I sensed from the beginning: this is *not* merely a 'plantswoman's garden' as it is called in the National Gardens Scheme yellow book; this is a garden where the consummate planter and the planner meet.

It seemed a problem garden when they bought it in 1974, so narrow, so long, so overhung with trees; the yew tree itself was a problem, dense and shaggy near the house. A tall and bushy neighbouring lilac cast its shade over the wall, and so did the venerable pear tree. At the far end a plane tree towered outside the back gate, but it might just as well have been inside the gate for all the protection they got from its leaves falling thick in autumn and covering everything. A third of the way down the garden, an old neglected pyracantha sprawled. Lucy found its orange berries 'harshly uninteresting'. There was the usual narrow path beside a too-narrow border running down the right-hand side.

They toyed with artful distractions from the garden's narrow length. Could they angle the axes, curve the paths? Could they follow Walpole's words when describing Pope's 'little bit of ground of five acres'? Pope, wrote Walpole, 'twisted and twirled and rhymed and harmonized this, till it appeared two or three sweet little lawns opening and opening beyond one another . . .'.

But Lucy wrote, in answer: 'The thin garden would not be twisted and twirled. The ogival curve applied to it – on our paper doodles – looked grotesque. The rhyming and harmonising principle was firmly lodged somewhere in our minds, though we did not see how to realise it, and so was the perspective principle, of views opening and opening.'

Once more, the idea of a circle supplied the answer, repeated circles supplied the rhyme. They paved a circle with concentrically laid bricks a third of the way down their strip. The diameter of the circle was almost the width of the garden; four small curved beds, the quadrants of the circle, were set in it; here in the middle stood the tall dark vase and here, at the side, was the seat where I sat in May facing south across the garden towards the pear tree. Propped against the garden wall opposite was a worn old headstone: you could just discern the letters underneath the lichen, recording the death of an eight-month baby in 1711. Two different, casual ferns and a self-seeded poppy sprang up at its feet. There was no more York paving beyond this point. The way on down the garden became lawn, with edging stones along the resumed boundary borders and the suggestion of a second circle, this time made of grass and edged with twin hedges of miniature box, beneath the gnarled and domed pyracantha tree. The low hedges were two arcs, each ending in a bastion of yew, and framing the vase of honeysuckle.

At this point it seemed the garden might be reaching its end, for beyond the pyracantha was a taller hedge, almost but not quite shutting off whatever lay beyond. It was made of *Elaeagnus x ebbingei*, beautiful in itself with shapely, silvery leaves. But beyond it opened up a final 'sweet little lawn' – a secret garden in the middle of which stood the specimen tree, the cercidiphyllum with its fresh green ovate leaves, its three stems giving it the air of a balanced work of art. Even at this

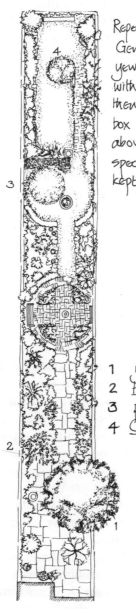

Repeated circles punctuate Lucy
Gent's long garden : first the
yew tree, then a circle of brick
with flower beds in the quadrants,
then a grass circle edged with
box, a domed pyracantha
above it, and finally the
specimen tree, a cercidiphyllum,
kept pruned to a neat sphere.

1　yew
2　Hydrangea villosa
3　pyracantha
4　Cercidiphyllum japonicum

final point, you could not tell where the end of the long garden came because now the tree blocked your view. It supplied the final circular statement of the garden: it grew from a round bed in the middle of the lawn, and was meticulously pruned each spring so that the circumference of its branches would not exceed that of its bed.

'It highlights tangible or measurable space,' Lucy wrote. 'All that meaningless air between parallel borders!'

When you did get round the tree and reached the garden's end you could not feel disappointed because here was a final visual pleasure: an oak bench at least 3.5m (12ft) long, with grand scrolled legs, placed hard up against the bricks, and seeming to fill the whole width of the garden and to have been tailormade for it (in fact it had been made redundant at Lucy's husband's place of work). It faced west, and invited you to sit down in the sun and look back. But if you did this, you could see only leaves. You were enclosed in a green space; you might have been in the country. It was an inspiration to put a beautiful bench against the warm brick wall where almost everyone else would assume there should be a flowerbed.

So now the garden has this other rhyme. It begins and ends with a tree: the dark yew at one end, the delicate cercidiphyllum at the other. Each dominates its space – one the sober stone paving, the other the fresh green grass. Nothing could be more different in character than the yew and the cercidiphyllum, but the simplicity of the statement in each case – a uniform ground colour and a rising tree – is the same. If you enter the garden from the house you think: 'How dignified, cool and spacious!' If you come in at the other end through the garden gate, you think: 'How secret, leafy and green!' A stranger standing at one end of the garden could have no suspicion of what the other end held in store. These two spaces, of the yew and the cercidiphyllum, mark the worlds of sun and shade in the garden. The yew rules the shady world it combines with the shadow of the high terraced houses to create. It is no longer the shaggy shapeless view-blocker it was when they came here. From time to time an expert prunes it of all its lower growths; a majestic trunk now rises bare for 6m (20ft) before any fuzzy foliage is allowed to break. Yew wood is pastel-tinted, almost more pink than brown; the bark is smooth and fluted so that you want to stretch out your hand and pat it as you pass. Then you have to pat the pottery disc below it.

'There is a sort of miasma beneath the yew,' Lucy said.

She applied herself to the subject of shade-loving plants. The raised bed of the yew is carpeted with variegated dead-nettle (*Lamium galeobdolon*), the indefatigable shade-carpeter with evergreen, ivory-etched leaves. It weeps round the pottery disc and over the retaining wall. Opposite, as a fringe to the big hydrangeas, are the other beautiful, well-known carpeters for dry shade: the epimediums (*E. x warleyense, E. x versicolor* 'Sulphureum', *E. perralderianum*) with delicate yellow flowers in May and heart-shaped fresh green leaves prettily poised on slender stems, tawny-bronze in autumn.

She was not after mere 'shade-survivors'. She wanted 'shade-flourishers', plants that would be at their best because of the shady place. This meant, in practice, woodland plants: camellias and rhododendrons, martagon lilies dangling their turk's-cap flowers over ferns, tiarella 'walking everywhere' she said, and the related tellima with leaves as round as a geranium's and spikes of lime-green bells rising through the bright, almost moist green leaves of *Daphne pontica* in May. Perhaps surprisingly, the luxuriant woodland planting seemed entirely in accord with the austere urban grandeur of the sweeping York paving and the dark, hand-thrown pots.

Daphne pontica is planted beyond *Hydrangea villosa*; where but in this garden would a daphne prove to have, not rosy flowers, but yellow ones? The rhododendrons are not the familiar towering and spectacular hybrid monsters, but dwarf species rhododendrons: *R. pseudochrysanthum* is half-hidden behind the daphne, its leaves a strange, dusty cocoa colour. On the edge of the path opposite, *Rhododendron yakushimanum*, though only 1m (3ft) tall, is a major beauty of the garden. It is a relatively new species, with profuse, voluptuous clusters of white flowers shaped like temple bells, followed by young biscuit-coloured leaves. All year, the undersides of its leaves are like soft chamois leather. If you are mischievous you can rub off some of the felting with your thumb and discover green beneath.

The camellias are unexpected too. 'Salutation' rather than 'Donation' grows here, a little more refined a pink, almost white in bud. Later comes the sumptuous double pink 'Leonard Messel'. There is a white one called 'Duccio's gem', whose petals in close-up are exquisitely faceted and faintly triangular, almost too perfect to be real. Another white hybrid, 'Cornish Snow', has small white semi-circle flowers, with golden stamens all along its branches, and when the flowers have fallen the new leaves turn prune-coloured as the light of summer strengthens.

Along the wall behind the camellias is what seems to be the old friend of London gardeners: *Hydrangea petiolaris*. But why do its leaves look elegantly pointed, and why are they grey-green underneath? The answer is that this is not *Hydrangea petiolaris* at all, but its relative *Schizophragma integrifolium*, which is also self-clinging, also has white hydrangea-like lacecap flowers in late summer, but is simply prettier, perhaps because you do not see it everywhere.

Nor do you see everywhere a wonderful spurge, slender and tall – almost 2m (6ft) – which dominates a stretch of the woodland border. It is *Euphorbia sikkimensis*, and its special distinction is the flame-red rib down the middle of each dull green leaf, and the flame red of its flower bracts in spring. For six months or more, this single plant catches the eye.

Then there are the shade-loving herbaceous plants which Lucy has collected. They tend to be tall, too; one can imagine them, in woodland, growing up in search of light. Tallest of all, at about 2m (6ft), and most graceful, is the bugbane, *Cimicifuga racemosa* 'Atropurpurea'. There is something slenderly resilient about its long stems and soft cream flower-spikes that makes it impervious to wind; to stake it would be an insult. Most people who have heard of cimicifuga grow a variety with green leaves not unlike the leaves of Japanese anemones, but the leaves on Lucy's variety are dull purple.

Nearby grows a clump of ligularia (*L. przewalskii*) with deeply incised basal leaves and wiry black stems, also soaring up to 1.5m (5ft) and topped by long golden flower-spikes. And behind the ligularia, against the wall, are the arching spines of Solomon's seal in a variegated form, and the straight, bright green fronds of hart's-tongue ferns. A few steps away a taller, bright green fern, *Matteuccia struthiopteris*, curls its fronds over like ostrich feathers.

Everywhere, arching stems complement straight stems. There are the strong, straight-stemmed rodgersias (*R. pinnata* 'Superba') with stiff, bronze, palmate leaves and stout raspberry-red stems and flowers; and then there is *Smilacena racemosa* whose forward movement is like that of its relative, Solomon's seal, but perhaps more 'rhythmic', Lucy says. There are beautiful flame-coloured day lilies (*Hemerocallis* 'Pink Damask') whose flower-stems are straight but whose rushy leaves arch; and of course there are true lilies (*Lilium henryi, L. martagon*), curving forwards as the petals of their trumpets curve backwards; and then there is the toad lily, *Tricyrtis formosana*, holding its small pink spotted flowers erect.

They need attentive care, all these beautiful perennials. Though they enjoy shelter from the sun, they don't enjoy shelter from the rain. They want water, food, and protection from slugs.

If you look for these plants in a garden centre you probably will not find many of them. If you look in a nurseryman's catalogue, you may find the genus, but not the particular variety Lucy grows. Often she finds them in small nurseries with photocopied lists. She visits great gardens; above all, she

visits Kew Gardens. She returns with details of treasure far
beyond the brown bearded irises I triumphantly noted when
I first visited Kew: *Kirengeshoma palmata*, for instance. 'Little
yellow shuttlecocks,' she says as we pass it. 'I saw it at Kew.'
But she does grow brown bearded irises too – the loveliest I
have ever seen – intense mahogany velvet, given to her by a
friend who was not quite sure of the name.

She does not collect rare plants for the sake of their rarity.
It is rather that she sees no point in duplicating plants that can
be enjoyed in other people's gardens, and she knows that there
are countless other lovely plants waiting to be used. She wants
the maximum return from each, the longest possible season of
flowering, or leaves as lovely as the flowers.

In the spring, the shaded woodland garden is a place
for spring flowers. First come snowdrops through hellebores;
then dog's-tooth violets (*Erythronium dens-canis*) push their
lovely reflexed petals in white and yellow through the carpet
of epimedium along with a purple fritillary, and snowflakes
(*Leucojum aestivum*) appear among the ostrich-feather ferns.
As the season advances and to the sun rises higher in the sky,
the interest of the garden spreads further east until by June
the second half of the garden, leading to the sunlit world of
the cercidiphyllum, is illuminated with roses.

'It seems to be mainly a rose garden,' said one of the
visitors on Open Day.

'Only in June,' I replied severely.

For the tide of flowers advances and retreats according to the
season. Plants you have never noticed on earlier visits seem to
rise and lean forward when their moment comes, while others
politely retire into supporting roles. It is like a large orchestra
where most instruments get their turn with the tune but then
combine to play the accompaniment. So, indeed, it is only in
June that the garden seems brimful of roses.

They are reassuringly familiar. If you go down to the bottom
of the garden to sit on the long bench there, the deep red 'Guinée'

flowers above your head, trained in horizontal lines along the wall. The healthy old rugosa 'Blanc Double de Coubert' is in the narrow border on your right, and the sturdy centifolia 'Fantin Latour' on your left. Above it, a high trellis fixed to the wall holds the famous climber 'Mme Grégoire Staechilin' whose enormous spread, and enormous perfumed pale pink roses, take the breath away before the rose season is in full swing. Across the grass is my old aunt's favourite rose, the alba 'Céleste', of the grey-green leaves and pointed buds and flat pink, camellia-shaped flowers. When it comes to roses, it is not a question of avoiding duplication; it is simply a question of trying to decide which is the loveliest.

The climbing roses along the walls seem to summarise all the favourite roses from other people's gardens in this story. Here is 'Paul's Lemon Pillar' which I thought of as my own. Here is 'Albertine' which I thought of as my daughter's. Here is 'Meg', the lovely single climber identified in a Grove Terrace front garden long ago. Here are 'Mme Alfred Carrière' and 'Zéphirine Drouhin' and 'New Dawn'. In all, eight great climbing roses decorate the garden.

Their abundance is deceptive. Lucy once said that *Gardening with String* should be the title of any gardening book she wrote, and all her roses are under vigilant supervision, skilfully trained and invisibly tied back with string (but never with 'twists' which cut fatally into the stems of roses). Through them and beside them twine over twenty cunningly controlled clematis that complement the colours of the roses. Pearly pink 'New Dawn' has lavender-blue 'Perle d'Azur' as its partner, with pink Japanese anemones growing in front; 'Guinée' shares its wall with the earlier, soft blue *Clematis alpina* 'Columbine'. White clematis frame 'Mme Grégoire Staechelin': the waxy 'Huldine' at one end and the large-flowered 'Marie Boisellot' at the other. There is a white clematis near 'Zéphirine Drouhin' too: *C. viticella* 'Alba Luxurians', whose small flowers have four sepals tipped with green. But the fiercely intense rose-madder of the thornless rose is more subtly neutralised by a very dark clematis at the other end of its spread, so deep a red as to be almost black in bud: the large-flowered 'Niobe'. *Clematis viticella* 'Rubra' grows between, the prodigality of its flowering nicely balanced by the smallness of each individual flower.

Roses and clematis overflow the borders and arch over the path. Looking down the garden from the house in summer, the eye is stopped by a pair of large shrub roses which bow to one another. On the right is *Rosa moyesii*, 2.7m (9ft) tall, wildly exuberant with ferny leaves and little single, blood-red flowers. To the left is *Rosa rubrifolia* (now *R. glauca*) whose name fluctuates like its leaf colour, purple-red overlaid with glaucous blue. The flamboyant arching of the first, and the duskily cool leaf colour of the second, make the little flowers on each one of secondary importance. The importance of these roses is their size, deliberately flaunting the school of thought which teaches that narrow gardens should be exclusively planted with small, neat shrubs.

A little nearer to the house grows a rose whose flamboyance lies in its flowering, a flowering that scarcely pauses for breath between June and September. It is the strange China rose 'Mutabilis', whose colours change from butter-gold through pink to raspberry red. Its single flowers have a flyaway air, the petals rather pointed, like pennants waving.

Beyond it, in one of the quadrant beds on the brick-paved circle, grows a little specimen that you look down on as you pass. It is perfectly neat: a dense posy of pure pink flowers. It rises from a wreath of blue-grey dicentra leaves (*Dicentra formosa* 'Langtrees') with white bells for flowers. It is not 'Petite de Holland', nor is it 'de Meaux', but it is a centifolia species: *R. centifolia* 'Parvifolia', and one is inclined to ask: 'Why have I never seen this rose before?' (see Plate 4).

Next comes a rose that I have seen before, in Tina's garden: the beautiful modern floribunda 'Margaret Merril', whose hugely double, almost frilly flowers are pale pink in the centre of the furled buds before they are quite open. Its young foliage has a handsome deep red tint, and its scent is heavy. Yet again, it is a case of: 'Why don't we all grow this?' It grows among delightfully unexpected neighbours. Towering over it and embracing it in strong silver arms is a massive *Phlomis fruticosa* with astonishing flowers like ruched rosettes of yellow velvet. In front of it grows a herbaceous paeony, 'Duchesse de Nemours', whose flowers are also huge and white, but muddled in the middle instead of folded, and held in outer guardian petals. 'It is like a beautiful white porcelain bowl,' said Lucy's husband, 'filled with a lovely pudding of whipped cream.' A humble feverfew, with white, yellow-centred daisy flowers, grows at the paeony's feet.

The garden is full of inspired groupings like this, where plants with odd resemblances as well as striking differences touch one another. A sure eye for a beautiful plant is one thing; a sure eye for which plants combine well together is another. The plant associations in this garden are at least as remarkable as the plants themselves. Lucy wishes that we gardeners could hold six plants together in our imaginations at once, but believes that, like blackbirds with their eggs, the most we can manage in our inward eye is three. The rest must be done by trial and error, experimenting on the ground. 'The garden is a laboratory,' she said when first she showed me round it, 'where I make mistakes.' She frequently moves plants about: 'It keeps them on their toes,' she says.

'Would the orange crocosmia look nice beside all these blue things?' she asks. (How flattering to be consulted.) Certainly some sunset-dinted *Alstroemeria ligtu* hybrids look stunning rising through purple salvia. She is adept at placing red-leaved plants. *Rosa rubrifolia* has the lovely pastel flowers of *Lavatera* 'Barnsley' (white tinged with pink) growing through it, and a dusky deep red clematis (*C. texensis* 'Gravetye Beauty') touches the silver and powder blue of *Teucrium fruticans* beyond. She has sunk a dashing lobelia with purple leaves and scarlet flowers (*Lobelia cardinalis* 'Queen Victoria') deep in the woodland border among dark and tawny leaves. The purple-leaved vine (*Vitis vinifera* 'Purpurea') is trained along the wall behind the silver-grey *Buddleia fallowiana* 'Alba' with pure white flowers, a delicate white poppy is at its feet, and the small, angular New Zealand shrub corokia with narrow, salty-looking grey-green leaves and a network of silver stems is tucked into a nearby corner. Silver is a catalyst that prevents discord in a garden. Little pools of silver freshen the flowerbeds. On one side is the Japanese 'painted fern', *Athyrium nipponicum metallicum*, which looks like silver filigree set with rubies, metallic, a mineral rather than a vegetable. A silver-leaved artemesia, *A. ludoviciana*, spreads beneath its fronds. On the brick paving, *Hebe pimelioides* 'Quicksilver' grows in a pot: beyond, *Artemesia* 'Powys Castle' and *Senecio leuchostachys* make different patterns of silver lace beside the deep green fleshy leaves of an *Acanthus mollis*. The clipped *Elaeagnus x ebbingei* hedge is touched with silver though there is pale green underneath, like salt sea-water under the surface of a breaking wave. To mark the hedge's end comes a more solidly green shrub: *Senecio rotundifolia*. Where the elaeagnus leaves are oval with a satin sheen, the senecio leaves are rounder, fleshier, frosted with white underneath.

It is such subtle contrasts, gentle colour modulations, that most characterise the garden; contrasts of leaf shape, leaf texture, huge thick leaves against sharp-cut ones, bright fresh greens against glaucous blues, or simply green against green. In summer, near the house, the sleek dark leaves of a well-fed skimmia contrast with a bright green fern; in winter, with the darker leaves of *Viburnum davidii* whose interest lies, not in gloss, but in the parallel tucks of its veins. There is not much yellow foliage in the garden, and for golden variegation only a few hostas. The variegation comes between one plant and its neighbour rather than on a single plant and thus shimmers to a gentler, dreamier rhythm.

In August, when most gardens look played out or dominated by harsh yellows, this garden is still fresh and cool. The roses may be largely over, but many clematis are in full, sumptuous flower – particularly two specimens of the semi-herbaceous *Clematis integrifolia* 'Durandii' which drape themselves over their neighbours and turn two stretches of a flower border into an intense, deep blue. Between them the pendant violet bells of *Clematis eriostemon* nod among the branches of *Ceanothus* 'Heavenly Blue', and near the house *Clematis* 'Jackmanii Alba' is producing its second batch of flowers, not double like its June display, but the large single white ones which were framing *Hydrangea villosa* on my first visit to the garden.

I now begin to know what all those August flowers of my first visit were. There is *Thalictrum dipterocarpum* 'Hewitt's Double' whose tall, ferny stems are topped by countless tremblingly delicate lilac balls; there is monarda, not the usual brazen red nor the vivid heliotrope, but a soft apricot pink; there is *Astrantia carniolica* 'Rubra', still flowering in green and old rose after two months; there is *Aster x frikartii* with mauve daisy flowers for weeks on end; and there is *Sedum spurium* 'Atropurpureum', with leaves that are not the usual sedum green, but purple-pink. Above all there are late lilies, standing in pots along the paving stones that edge the lawn. The colours are strange and delicate, and include one of Dr North's hybrids named after mythological characters: 'Eros', the colour of strawberries and cream; a hybrid tiger lily of soft yellow called 'La Bohème', and a luscious trumpet called 'Redstart' which is not strident scarlet, as its name suggests, but garnet.

'Why do you have so many pots?' asks a visitor.

'Because I have run out of space,' says Lucy.

She does not say: 'Because they look nice,' but they do. The series of dark pots by Jenny Lloyd Jones are part of the garden's essential beauty. The tallest of them all stands by the back door, with assorted humbler pots grouped round it, each with a group of hostas drooping their leaves over the edge. The largest pot holds the small-leafed, slug-resistent *Hosta tardiflora*; slightly higher, in a smaller pot, is *Hosta tardiana* 'Halcyon'; beside it are assorted hostas with ivory-striped leaves. Their cool flowers are out in August and September.

When autumn comes the garden is still not primarily yellow – or rather the yellow leaves shine through a rosy glow of pink and red mixed with blue-grey. Three slender trees have been planted for their autumn leaves, to save the garden from the sad sense that the show is over in November. They do not spread, and they do not cast much shade, for their leaves are delicate. There is *Amelanchier canadensis* which turns a brilliant flame; there is *Gleditsia triacanthos* 'Ruby Lace' with pinnate leaves which turn redder and redder the more the late sun shines. Best of all there is a choice rowan: *Sorbus hupehensis* obtusa, whose ferny leaves turn incandescent coral ('pears in red wine,' Lucy calls them) a day or two before they fall; the berries are not orange-red but muted, dull green overlaid with pink. Between the sorbus and gleditsia, against the wall, is the most brilliant of all autumn shrubs: a fothergilla, with intensely scarlet leaves. Meanwhile, at the bottom of the garden, the leaves of the cercidiphyllum are turning from soft green to smoky pink and yellow; near the house *Euphorbia griffithii* is mixing its yellow with coral and red, and the towering *Euphorbia sikkimense* is now subsiding in swathes of gold, still touched with red and green. The flowers on *Hydrangea villosa* are all dusky burnt rose among grey leaves.

Everywhere pinks and reds are complemented by washes of grey-blue in the leaves of senecios, artemesias and dicentras, and a tiny pine tree, *Pinus beauvronensis*, planted by the end of the stone path, comes into its own when the roses of *Rosa chinensis* 'Mutabilis' fall: it is a plump buttress of soft blue-green needles scarcely 1m (3ft) tall.

There is just the right skeleton structure of evergreens in

the garden to stop it looking bare when winter comes; the yew towers dark and protective near the house, with its bed of familiar sage-green lamium beneath it; halfway down the garden the pyracantha leans on a wooden prop, and when the rich planting round it has waned, the patterns made by its gnarled and twisted stems show up like a tree painted on a Chinese plate. Its rounded top is pruned to echo the round brick paving below it, whose complete circle is clearer now that the edging plants have died back and some pots have been moved indoors for the winter. At each end of the long bench is an evergreen: a tall, dark eucryphia and a noble *Viburnum rhytidophyllum* with huge, sombre leaves which manage to look both soft and stiff at the same time, and are as ribbed as the leaves of the small *Viburnum davidii* near the house. Then there are the dwarf rhododendrons, the dwarf pine and the skimmias. Suddenly the evergreen *Clematis armandii* is importantly present, its leathery three-lobed leaves along the wall beside the back door and over the door itself; a second specimen spreads wide halfway down the garden, showering its wall with winter stars. By February, hellebores are opening along the borders.

It emerges that all the loveliest winter flowers have found a place here. Outside a ground-floor window and arching over the small garden shed, *Prunus subhirtella* 'Autumnalis' bursts into bloom. Again close to the house, a *Viburnum x bodnantense* 'Dawn' flowers profusely so that, between the prunus and the viburnum, this end of the garden is arched with pink and white winter blossom; you look down into it from the bathroom window. On the far side of the great shrubby hydrangeas is a *Hamamelis mollis*, not the usual yellow but a variety called 'Carmine Red'. Far down the garden beyond the hedge an enviable winter sweet (*Chimonanthus praecox*) flowers generously against a south wall. The garden passes the Miss Jekyll test: not only through its plants, but through the shapely order of its paving, its pots, its lawns, its hedges and trees, it is beautiful in winter.

In spring the effects are different. Because the choice is wider, there is more room for surprise. There are no forsythia, no spring-flowering fruit trees in this strip, for they still bloom in all the other terrace gardens over the walls. But the young leaves of the cercidiphyllum open pink; they shine in the light. In March the lovely shrub of early spring, *Corylopsis pauciflora*, opens its pale yellow scented flowers which are poised on its branches as delicately as the flowers of the winter sweet. In May there are tulips and wallflowers. The wallflowers are not bedded, but perennials in pots: *Cheiranthus* 'John Codrington', a mixture of dusty pink and amber; and the tulips are not bright; they are an old variety called 'Bleu Aimable' – loveable but not blue, rather a soft, streaked lavender, fading to silver as they age.

Now the paeonies begin to open: the unpronounceable, unforgettable *P. mlokosewitschii*, modest in height but a braggart in flower, with single cups of lemon yellow; then a wild one from seed with small red flowers; a huge familiar tree paeony, *P. lutea ludlowii* beyond the pyracantha; finally, beside the long oak bench, my own old hybrid tree paeony, 'Mrs William Kelway', opens her unbelievable white double flowers. It is too much. How can there be room for *everything* in this garden?

And there is more. There is another daphne, *Daphne odora*, beside the back gate; as if there were not already four viburnums, there is a lovely May-flowering pink one, *Viburnum nudum* 'Pink Beauty', chosen, understandably, for its modest size. And as if the two huge hydrangeas were not enough, there are *H. quercifolia*, the oak-leaved hydrangea with scalloped leaves, and *H. paniculata*, with cones of creamy flowers.

Earlier, I toyed with the idea that every plant here is equal, that every plant gets its turn in the spotlight. Now I begin to believe that there are star performers, because of a show stopper that flowers in June. It is *Carpenteria californica*.

It frames the south-facing seat, warmly placed against the wall for it is said to be not hardy. On Open Day it was another case of: 'What's *that*!' for it was spectacularly smothered in waxy flowers: big, scented, ivory flowers in clusters of five, each with five petals arranged round golden stamens; it seemed like orange blossom seen through a magnifying glass and, like orange blossom, the flowers were set among bright green leaves. A *Clematis texensis* 'Etoile Rose', with cerise-pink bell-shaped flowers, twined through it. (See Plate 4.)

I start to make a checklist of other star performers in the cast: *Hydrangea villosa* of course, and the yew tree, and the cercidiphyllum, and the little pine; then the dwarf white rhododendron and the tall green euphorbia; the wonderful white *Clematis* 'Jackmanii alba', and the two blue herbaceous *Clematis integrifolia* 'Durandii'; then all the roses. . . . It is absurd; the list goes on and on without a moment's pause. It seems to be, after all, an all-star cast.

Yet there *are* lesser players in the garden. They are the uninvited ones, the self-seeders. They fill their usual crucial role, spreading a relaxed sense of spontaneity here, just as they did in my so-called 'untidy gardens'. There are columbines, 'grannies' bonnets', in purple and pink, joining the great pale group of white rose and paeony, lavatera and phlomis. There are bellflowers, campanulas, not only pushing through *Hydrangea villosa*, but everywhere. Between the tiled path and the lawn are occasional clumps of self-sown acid-green feverfew and *Alchemilla mollis*, and the tiny pink and white daisy, *Erigeron mucronatus*. Yellow Welsh poppies dare to grow round the cercidiphyllum bed, and a selected number are allowed to do so. Alliums explode their fireworks. The closely related *Nectaroscordum cyculum* dangles its bells, like miniature Victorian glass lampshades. A white foxglove rises through silver teucrium. Cranesbills with flowers ranging from pinky white to reddish black (*Geranium phaem*) spread over the brick paving. The deep purple leaves of *Viola labradorica* appear beneath the ferny blue-green foliage of *Dicentra eximia* 'Stuart Boothman', while the small striped *Saxifraga cuscutiformis* makes its own colonies by spreading underground roots.

Of course you do not see the soil anywhere among the dense planting of the garden. Nor do you see the edges of the beds. For all you know, the left-hand border may have a low retaining wall, for it seems to be higher than the path. In fact there is no retaining wall; it is simply that the soil is piled up high. In the one bare corner of the garden, just underneath a ground-floor window of the house, there is a neat pile of sacks with a narrow roof above them: six different sorts of peat and hop manure are waiting. But when Lucy is asked *how* she does it, how she can grow so many plants so close together, she becomes vague.

'Bonemeal,' she murmurs, 'though it's old-fashioned now.'

'Don't you use Growmore in the spring?' I enquire.

'Oh yes.' Then she adds: 'Hop manure is very good.'

She has no compost heap; she does not know where she could put it. She has no greenhouse; she says she does not know what she would do with all the plants she would raise. The fact is that she cannot spare the space; she needs it for her plants.

Her interest in them is passionate. She has the discriminating eye of the collector and the creative eye of the artist; she is a wonderfully skilful pruner; her plants are shapely and strong. It is no good thinking that one of her star plants would look equally good if planted in isolation in someone else's garden.

Yet she does have her unsuccesses. Her beautiful schyzophragma spreads wide and leafy, but does not flower. Her 'Nevada' shrub rose sickened, so she cut it down, but it meant that the lovely little tree which grew behind it, *Styrax japonica*, with flowers like snowdrops in June, could be more fully seen. Surprisingly, her *Magnolia stellata* does not flower either.

'Perhaps it doesn't like having a clematis growing over it?' I murmured.

'It has that as a punishment,' she replied.

Always she takes this amused, unruffled attitude towards her plants. She never grumbles or apologises; she loves them and is tolerant of their idiosyncrasies. She also tolerates the lordly behaviour of her three cats, who think they own the garden. She never seems tired or dirty.

In country gardens, she says, you see plants against the sky. In town gardens, you see plants against each other. But that May there was a metamorphosis: the sun shone every day and it was hard to remember what rain was like. We looked upwards at an arching bramble (*Rubus x tridel* 'Benenden') high above the elaeagnus hedge, and saw its single white flowers like large, wild roses against the blue sky.

Everything I have longed to find, as well as things I did not know I wanted, come together in this garden. The balance between pattern and profusion is its key motif. Lucy paraphrases that balance by quoting a line from Vita Sackville-West: 'Maximum formality with maximum informality.' But here the idea ceases to be a paradox, a tension between opposites, and becomes, instead, a fusion. The formality is swallowed up by the informality; the planting is the pattern.

XII

Window-box and Chimneypot

Sweet Spring, full of sweet days and roses
A box where sweets compacted lie. . . .

George Herbert, 'Virtue'

This does not feel like gardening; it is more like cooking. I have lifted the window-box in from the sill and on to the kitchen table, spooned out the surface soil to a depth of 7.5cm (3in), and spiked the compacted dry earth below (full of fibrous white root filaments), with a long-handled three-pronged kitchen fork. I have damped the new John Innes No. 3 potting compost in a big discarded baking dish, stirring the water in more easily here than if I were trying to do it in the window-box itself. I have buried six bulbs of the miniature narcissus 'W.P. Milner' at the bottom of the box; above and between them I have pressed into the damp compost the clustered bulbs of pale pink multiflora hyacinths; I have been gradually building up the compost as I go, never quite covering one layer of bulbs till the next is in place, so that I can see what I am doing. The top layer is composed of twenty-four little bulbs of *Crocus chrysanthus* 'Blue Bird' about 5cm (2in) from the top. Now I shall put them in the bottom of a dark cupboard for a month or two. It is my window-box for next spring.

This small, earthenware trough on the kitchen window-sill and a tall black chimneypot on the front doorstep are my town garden now. The chimneypot was standing with a whole company of others on the pavement in the square where we now live, after workmen had remade a neighbouring roof. Through the window I watched people drive up, select a likely pot and drive away with it. When I'd been watching for a while I thought I'd like to help myself to one. By then, only two comparative duds remained. I took the black one, which seemed to have started out as cheerful red and been smudged over at some time with bituminous roof paint. It has now been standing on our north-facing doorstep, three steps away from the street, for three years, but no one has yet taken a fancy to it. There is something to be said for choosing the dud.

In it grows a sarcococca – a shrub which used to flourish in Australian gardens though it comes from China – given to me as a present when it was quite small. Its other name is 'sweet box'. It is evergreen, with leaves that are much narrower than box leaves and more pointed. It likes the shade and it flowers in winter; the flowers are tiny, tubular, white fringed with pink, and sweetly scented. No one has yet taken a fancy to it either, but it pleases me. I planted it in an old 23cm (9in) black plastic pot, then found that this pot fitted exactly inside the circumference of the chimneypot. It has decided to grow quite erect and formal, in accord with our black front door. It is now two years old, and 60cm (2ft) tall. Its maximum height is said to be 90cm (3ft); luckily it is the variety *S. hookeriana digyna* which is smaller than the type.

Other people fill their chimneypots with rubble to a halfway mark, then with good potting soil. Some people fill them with soil from bottom to top. (But our front step has the space of a basement area beneath it, and perhaps is better without the extra weight of soil.) And other people grow trailing things, or arching things, in their chimneypots: small-leaved ivies, or small-flowered species clematis (*C. macropetala* or *C. alpina*) or dangling fuchsias or trailing geraniums or periwinkles or ferns. Tina grows three or four different plants (a lily, an ivy, a cordyline and a euonymus) all inside a single chimneypot.

The capacity of plants to adapt themselves to root restriction astonishes me. So long as they have food and water, they seem inclined to live. At least, I hope this is true, because now I do not want to be without an amiable, neat, dark sarcococca on my doorstep.

The kitchen window faces south. I have brought my spring box out of its cupboard because the tips of the bulbs are showing. In February the first crocuses open wide when the sun touches them and there is a close-up view through the window-pane of their saffron-orange stigma and of the dark violet brushstrokes down the back of each petal. The flowering continues for about five weeks, but when the last flowers are finished, shrivelled and capsized, the striped leaves grow long and make a soft, unobtrusive basis round the hyacinths which are just starting to flower in sugar pink, fading to shell pink with age; the close-up view through the window shows a starfish of deeper pink marked in the middle of each floweret. Open the window on a sunny March morning and the scent pours into the kitchen. Unfortunately opening the window is a performance: you have to climb a chair and unscrew the burglar catches first. This performance makes all tending of the window-box a slight chore.

When the hyacinths are fading the daffodils start to open. They should be slightly taller than the hyacinths – about 30cm (10in) high but not too tall or large-flowered, or they will look inappropriate and top-heavy. The 45cm (18in) trumpet daffodils that lean forwards from grand West End window-boxes between skimmias and variegated laurels (now reinstated in a new role as window-box shrubs) look uncomfortable. But my pretty, pale narcissus 'W.P. Milner' proves to be too short, no taller than the fading hyacinths. I should have gone for the 35cm (14in) 'Peeping Tom', but I did not like its name nor what the name stood for: an extra long and snoopy trumpet. Other famous cyclamineus narcissi with blown-back petals, 'February Gold' or 'February Silver', would be the right height, and as their flowers seem almost impervious to age and weather, blooming for at least a month, they might well predate and outlast the hyacinths and prove to be the ideal narcissi for window-boxes. Some of my 'W.P. Milner' have turned out to be blind. The disappointment is depressing; there is no room for failures in a window-box. I have dug out all the spring bulbs and replanted them in the country, and brought some rejects from the country and planted them in town.

The rejects are pansies and violas whose colours were unacceptable in the bed where they grew: coronation colours of purple and claret and gold. But I still find it difficult to confiscate healthy plants altogether, dumping them on the compost heap because their colours clash. Massed together in a box on a London windowsill, I can easily persuade myself that they look rich and choice.

Violas are lovely plants for close-up viewing; they obligingly turn their faces to the glass and look in, as well as out. The etched lines that radiate from the central petals of my 'Jackanapes' violas are like the whiskers a child draws on a cat's face. There are five petals; the top two are rounded rather like Micky Mouse's ears. Yet despite these nursery associations, violas have refinement. There is no need to mix them with other plants unless the window-box is big. My small Italian trough needs nothing in early summer but violas elbowing each other, jockeying amiably for position among themselves, and holding up their flowers on delicate stems from end to end of the box. Continual dead-heading and watering are now the tasks. We return from the country after three hot days of early May and find the violas splayed out, exhausted, all the flowers dead, the dry centre of each plant showing, and a telltale feather suggesting that a pigeon has been roosting in the window-box. I stick some butcher's skewers into the soil, sharp end upwards, to serve as plant props and bird-scarers at the same time. A complete dead-heading and watering puts the plants back in business by the next morning. But perhaps, after all, violas are an imperfect choice for a south-facing window-box whose owners tend to go away for three days at a time. The moment comes when the leggy remains of mine go down the waste-disposal unit.

So what should my summer choices be? The easy answers lie all round me in neighbouring streets. Just as gardeners learn best from other people's gardens, so window-gardeners learn from other people's window-boxes.

The first thing I have learnt is that clashing colours don't seem to clash in window-boxes. Just round the corner of the square are two boxes cram-full of cyclamen-pink busy lizzies, scarlet geraniums, a pale pink fuchsia, deep blue lobelia and bright orange African marigolds. I have tended to the view that orange marigolds clash with almost everything, yet here they are packed in among the pinks and reds and getting away with it. What's more, they give the box a sort of lift; it is a miniature version of the dazzling bedding in the square garden opposite, more refreshing to the eye than the plain row of scarlet geraniums edged with white alyssum in the window-box next door.

The second thing I have learnt follows from the first: window-boxes look best when they are crammed with flowers. Five scarlet geraniums in a row interspersed with four white alyssum is not enough, though we are tempted to say 'that will be enough' when we are shopping at a plant stall. Bare soil in a border is a pity; in a window-box it is a disgrace. Moreover, most window-boxes are plastic because plastic is light and cheap, and their sides need to be hidden by sprawlers. To see nothing but flowers and foliage along the windowsill is the ideal. Small-leafed ivies are supreme because they are easy, put up with drought, are prepared to send graceful festoons trailing a yard long below the windowsill, come in many pale and pretty variegations, and are still there in winter. A box where nothing survived but rampant trailing ivy looked better to my eye as I walked the streets than a box with five upward-growing leggy annuals in it and nothing else.

The third thing I have learnt is that you can score an easy win by matching your window-box to the paint-work of your house. Even more than a front garden, a front window-box is an architectural appendage. A box fringed with intense blue lobelia matched a royal blue front door; white marguerites matched a white one.

Suddenly I saw that the fashions prevailing in gardens could be transferred to window-boxes. Where Sissinghurst had its white garden, I could have a white window-box. I saw one in the front window of a north-facing terrace cottage: it was full of white impatiens with slightly taller white *Begonia semperflorens* at the back. Just as in a garden, I could use studied discords, shaded harmonies, or single colours. I could have any colour scheme I wanted, or none.

But when it came to the flowers I might work with, it was a different story. Judging by the summer boxes all round me, the roll call of window-box flowers was short. For the shade there were impatiens, *Begonia semperflorens*, violas and fuchsias; for the sun there were petunias, geraniums, nasturtiums, and African marigolds; for both there was lobelia, pale blue, dark blue or white. I loved the shady boxes; I looked down into a dark basement and saw a trough tight-packed with scarlet busy lizzies which must have rejoiced the hearts of the people who looked out from that basement room as much as they did the passer-by. I loved to see the pale pink trailing fuchsia mixed with *Begonia semperflorens*; I saw the miraculous performance of multicoloured impatiens heaped into domes of colour: white with pink centres among scarlet and cyclamen, all happy together with frills of dark blue lobelia in between. Continuous colour is what window gardening – or street gardening – is about; there is no room for an off-season. Because the available space is so small, the colours must be intensely concentrated. It is for this reason that half-hardy plants win the day – the plants that started life in heated greenhouses. Brilliant and ephemeral, they are prepared to flower their heads off all summer long and then be swept away.

They move into the garden centres in late April and early May in neat polystyrene strips – petunias, snapdragons, nemesias, lobelias – all joined together with sticky tape. 'Mixed Colours', the labels used to say. Now they are beginning to say 'yellow' or 'pink' or 'white' – an important advance for the window gardener who wants to work out a colour scheme, and who used to be forced to buy more expensive pot-grown plants to be certain of the right colour. The geraniums, of course, will be pot-grown: two or three will be enough, placed among other things. They are virtually indispensable for the sunny box belonging to the faithless householders who tend to go away.

> The reminiscence comes
> Of sunless dry geraniums
> And dust in crevices . . .

wrote T.S. Eliot in 'Rhapsody on a Windy Night', making us all seem to recognise a memory. But his geraniums belong to some neglected room or greenhouse from which the gardener has long since moved on. Sunny dry geraniums will flower. They don't have to be scarlet; they can be salmon pink, or magenta, or white splashed with fuchsia, or simply chalk white. They don't have to be strongly upward-growing: they can be ivy-leaved, small-flowered and trailing, taking the place, in summer boxes, of ivy itself. Like the trailing 'Elegante' their leaves can be variegated, green and white with astonishing pink round the edges. Or, once more, they can be mixed colours, thrilling clashes all in a single box. It was a bed of clashing geraniums that first brought the great garden designer Russell Page to the notice of Stéphane Boudin, the interior designer. In *The Education of a Gardener* (Collins, 1962) Page described planting 'orange-scarlet, crimson, vermilion, salmon and magenta geraniums spiced with enough white to make these clashing reds vibrate together.'

The best plants for window-boxes are the plants which look better in window-boxes – or containers – than anywhere else. Geraniums head the list: stuck into a space in a garden flowerbed they look aliens, uncomfortable stop-gaps; in urns, boxes or flower-pots they look regally at home.

I would be happy to mix pink geraniums with white marguerites and silver *Helichrysum petiolatum* or ivy on my windowsill in summer. All these would hang on bravely in dry conditions during my absences. But there is the nagging urge to be different, to find slightly original mixtures for window-boxes – perhaps less well adapted but also less clichéd.

In quest of ideas and discoveries, I queued up at Chelsea to see the entrants in the Window-box Competition. The queue was long; window-boxes draw the crowds. When I reached the exhibit there were no discoveries, only the old, tight-packed prettiness at its very best: more half-hardy annuals, with ivy and geraniums, in a series of enviably capacious 1m (3ft) boxes. They were all planted to be viewed from the street, not from the window; they turned their backs on the imagined householder and their faces towards the Chelsea crowds.

All the colour schemes were there again. Mirroring the white and silver gardens of our day was a grey and white window-box (white daisies among lacy-leafed artemesias); then there were two-colour boxes where white was mixed with one other colour: white with yellow (white petunias, daisies and begonias, yellow mimulus, violas, creeping jenny, and gold-splashed ivy); white with pink (with glamorous two-toned pelargoniums among pearl-pink and white begonias, pink verbena and silver helichrysum); scarlet with white (creamy violas among scarlet geraniums, with artemesia at the back and pale ivy at the front). Further on, the deep red and purple borders of Hidcote were echoed in a box where purple and magenta petunias mingled with purple and red fuchsias;

shaded pastel borders found their counterparts in a box where tiny lemon-yellow violas mixed with pale blue felicia, and pale pink fuchsias and cranesbill mixed with rosemary.

But one box was a herb garden. A little bay tree in the middle gave structure and shape; beside it grew feathery fennel, and towards the front, borage with its bright blue flowers, chives and marjoram; tiny purple velvet heartsease violas peeped through the herbs along with 'Alaska' nasturtiums, whose orange, scarlet and amber flowers glowed among cream-splashed leaves. How long the bay tree could survive in these cramped quarters I did not know. It might well be regarded as expendable, like annuals – or like the brave but tender cordyline which dominated a nearby exotic window-box where indoor plants had moved outside for the summer.

There was only one box that aimed at an illusion of permanence. This was symmetrically planted with three dwarf junipers rising from a groundwork of trailing ivy and limestone chips: a French formal garden in a window-box. Or was it a demonstration of what can be done in winter?

Winter boxes are a problem, if you want to get away from the ivy and the ubiquitous dwarf conifers. I do want to get away from the conifers. Everyone has plants that they dislike: my dislike is of dwarf conifers, and my strong dislike is of golden dwarf conifers, followed by conifers of glaucous blue. It is a strange thing that plants arouse such vehement antipathies – such passionate hatreds as well as loves.

'I hate dahlias!' is a familiar cry. It carries with it something like a moral condemnation of those who grow them. For hand in hand with the entrenched prejudices goes a sort of gardening snobbery that suggests those who *like* the thing you loathe are not only wrong, but vulgar.

'I hate begonias!' says one.

'I hate ferns!' says another.

Or, spreading the net wider: 'I hate variegated plants!' cries a third. 'I hate double flowers!' rejoins a fourth. One friend declares she hates geraniums; another hates petunias, another tulips.

What hope remains for window-boxes if all these vetoes are observed? Half-hardy annuals have a particularly hard time of it when the plant prejudices close in. Yet I notice that the more knowledgeable the gardener, the wider and more tolerant the taste. For they are a matter of taste, these preferences. There are no ultimate rights and wrongs in the matter, and no single correct answer to any gardening problem, even in a window-box.

The Victorians thought they knew all the answers. They often used the word 'tasteful', with the implication that some people had taste and others had not. I have been reading a small book called *The New Practical Window Gardener* by John R. Mollison, published in 1877. The pages still burst with ideas, and flowers. For example, the author envisages 'a tasteful little rockery, built up on your windowsill, so that your window-box may act as the crowning point of it.' He strongly recommends training climbing plants all round the window from either end of the box, clinging to twine which you attach to nails hammered into crevices in the mortar. Sweet peas could be trained up it, or climbing nasturtiums, or Scarlet Runner beans or canary creeper (*Tropaeolum peregrinum*). He envisages the seeds of hardy annuals, clarkia, candytuft, baby blue eyes (nemophila) and mignonette, sown in patches between geraniums, for he keeps a careful eye on cost as well as an appreciative one on colour. Pastels and monotone schemes do not speak to him: he likes the warm, rich Victorian palette of crimsons and purples, browns and golds; brilliance is what he is after in the grimy streets of nineteenth-century London – brilliance, and symmetry. The ends of the box must balance each other, and something must mark the middle. He writes:

'Now supposing ... you have got your window-box in beautiful array, and the graceful creepers twining bower-like around the window, what would be prettier than a neat wire basket hanging from the centre, with a creeper twining round the wirework and hanging down in little festoons of flower and foliage, a bright Scarlet Geranium and a plant or two of Blue Lobelia filling it up within? Such a window would create quite a sensation in the neighbourhood.

He urges the planting of a window-box in a philanthropic spirit: 'I hold that every person who has a flower in his window confers a benefit on the town at large.' He is right. I have felt the benefit of bright window-boxes, and have also noted that most houses do not have window-boxes at all.

But my window-box is primarily for me. It is to look at from inside as it does not face the street. I am experimenting with untidiness. I have deliberately planted a weed: oxalis, with pretty clover leaves and tireless small pink flowers; I admired it growing lavishly in a friend's front tubs and she gave me a seedling in a polythene bag to carry home. It seemed to languish and die, but one day some fresh green leaves appeared above the compost. For a moment I thought: how did that weed get into my window-box? But then I remembered that it must be my oxalis and felt pleased. Now I watch it grow. It has four three-lobed leaves and I wait for its cochineal-pink flowers. If, one day, it threatens to take over the box, I can always dig it out. The box is wildly asymmetrical because osteospermum, raised by another gardening friend, grows vigorously at the other end, ever branching and budding. These two plants, one quite tall, and one quite short, are episodes at either end of the pottery trough. But the theme of my summer box is to be herbs, for this is a sunny kitchen windowsill and I have nowhere else to grow them. The colour of my summer box will be green.

I have started with two rooted cuttings of scented-leafed geranium. Their flowers are insignificant, pale pink, but their leaves smell of rose petals and the light shines through them, making them translucent lettuce-green. I count them as herbs because they can be used to flavour iced summer puddings. They are growing steadily in the warmth, plump and neat; presently they may grow over the edge of the box and begin to trail a little. Close by, a plant of common thyme with tiny dull leaves and tiny washed-out flowers is already growing over the rim and doing the job that ivies do in orthodox window-boxes. Behind the thyme is a plant of chives. So far its leaves are behaving themselves and growing straight and tall, instead of breaking over halfway up as the chives do in my country garden. These chives in my window-box perform the function of a clump of irises in a mixed border: the slender verticals save the mass of ordinary leaf shapes from monotony.

But I have not actually got a *mass* of ordinary leaf shapes; my box (or trough) is a bare 43cm (17in) long. So far it contains the scented-leafed geranium, the osteospermum, the oxalis, the thyme and the chives. Two patches of bare earth remain, and when it rains the earth from these patches splashes up on to the window-pane. Of course I could cover the surface with pea-gravel to prevent this, as I do in spring before the bulbs are fully grown. But unhesitatingly I shall follow the rule of profusion and fill my spaces with plants. And here the old fun of gardening returns: what shall they be, these two chosen plants, which herbs would be best? Should they be chosen with cooking in mind, or should they be chosen for their looks? My answer is: one of each. Bright green, succulent-leafed basil for the kitchen; a seedling of feverfew for its pretty, fresh, white, yellow-centred flowers. If I can find a feverfew seedling with golden leaves so much the better, to contrast with the prevailing greens. And I plan to sow nasturtium seeds between the herbs, 'Alaska' or 'Whirlybird Mixed'. I shall not be bored with those big wrinkled seeds, as I was in my Melbourne childhood.

But it still isn't real gardening, this window-box business. It feels now, as I select herbs for spaces, more like flower-arrangement, filling spaces in a vase. I have a little trowel, as well as my kitchen fork. I have a big jug, kept full of water at room temperature, sometimes with a small pinch of phostrogen in it. I water the box quite often, though not every day. I stand there inside the room and only my hands are gardening.

Real gardening involves your whole body, your feet as well as your hands, your knees, your shoulders and your back. It submerges you and tires you; you reach upwards, stretch forwards, bend, kneel, push and pull. At the end of the day you fall asleep in your chair. Window-gardening is not tiring enough.

Real gardening involves most of your thoughts, too, while you are doing it. Perhaps because it is strenuous and physically demanding, it does not leave you much spare energy for dwelling on the problems that are teasing you at other times of day. You do not live in the past while you are gardening, nor spend much time on self-reproach or regret. It asks concentration: you have to keep your eyes open and your mind on what you are doing. But window-gardening only occupies a fraction of your attention for about five minutes at a time.

You are not lonely when you garden. You work with an accomplice, nature; or rather, you are the accomplice, nature the driving force. There is not enough scope for nature's way of working in a window-box.

Gardens carry constant worries, but they are manageable ones – vegetable worries, as slow as Marvell's 'vegetable love'. 'What is the matter with my clematis?' is cool speculation compared with: 'What is the matter with my child?' There are deaths and disappointments, of course, because gardening deals with life. When I revisit the gardens I have described, I find fatalities have happened everywhere. I ask to see the 'Papa Meilland' rose and Serafina replies: 'I haven't *got* "Papa Meilland" any more.' I ask where the tulips 'Bleu Aimable' are growing and Lucy says: 'They didn't *do* this year.' Gardening is a battle with retreats as well as victories.

But it is not the retreats and victories that are important. The state of mind of the gardener is what matters. This state of mind is compounded of hope and wonder. You sow your seeds with hope; then there is a moment of wonder when, weeks later, you find that they are flowering.

Index

179